HAUNTED VIRGINIA CEMETERIES

SHARON PAJKA

Published by Haunted America
A division of The History Press
An imprint of Arcadia Publishing
Charleston, SC
www.historypress.com

First published 2025

Manufactured in the United States

ISBN 9781467157209

Library of Congress Control Number: 2025937577

Notice: The information in this book is true and complete to the best of our knowledge. It is offered without guarantee on the part of the author or The History Press. The author and The History Press disclaim all liability in connection with the use of this book.

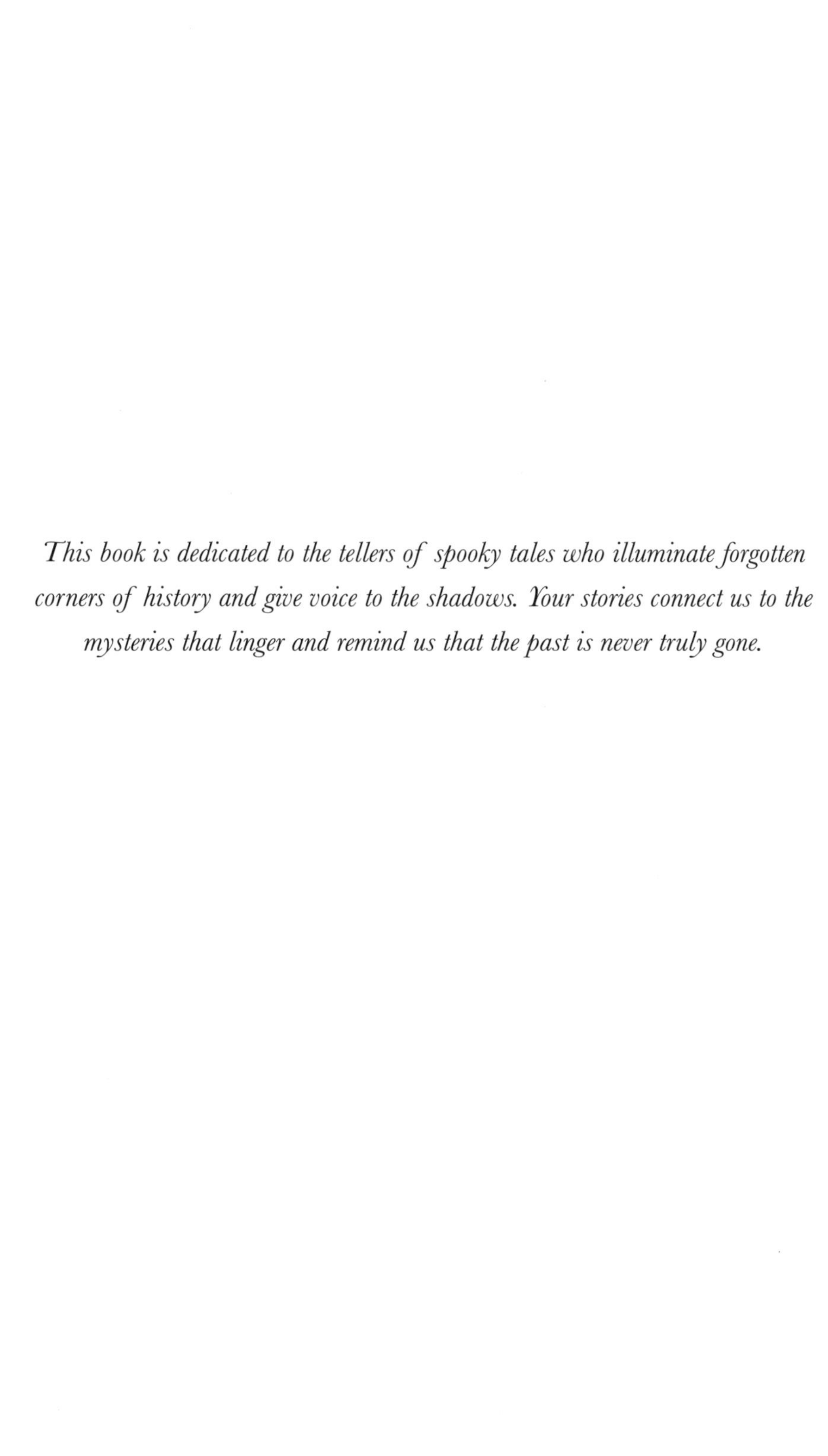

This book is dedicated to the tellers of spooky tales who illuminate forgotten corners of history and give voice to the shadows. Your stories connect us to the mysteries that linger and remind us that the past is never truly gone.

CONTENTS

Acknowledgements

I am grateful to those who have generously contributed to this project, especially the newspaper reporters, librarians, archivists, historians, tour guides and cemetery associates who shared their time and knowledge—your assistance made this thematic tour of Virginia cemeteries so much fun. To the storytellers who have passed down spooky tales of mystery and intrigue, thank you for preserving the spirit of the unknown.

Special thanks to the universities and institutions that offered access to their archives and to the individuals who graciously shared personal stories and insights. Your willingness to help unearth the past has been invaluable.

Without the encouragement, support and feedback from Johnathan Shipley, this project would not have been brought to life.

INTRODUCTION

I wouldn't give a hoot for anybody who doesn't believe in ghosts.
—Reverend Dr. W.A.R. Goodwin[1]

The scariest place I recall from my childhood is the old graveyard behind Emmaus Baptist Church in New Kent. It is in the country; there are no streetlights other than the porch lights of the nearby buildings. The church is a Greek Revival building with a gable roof. Approximately forty feet away is a recreational building. Both buildings are surrounded by woods. I visited that property for over a decade, mostly in the evenings for Girl Scout meetings. Inside the recreational hall, we crafted and strategized earning badges and selling cookies. The formal ceremonies were held next door in the church. After our weekly meetings, we played games and ran around the front lawn.

Walking down the sidewalk that connects the buildings, my eyes played tricks while glancing toward the trees, and I could just barely see the gravestones and that gnarled old oak tree, which I believed beckoned little children to come closer. The graveyard was not fenced, and while walking along the sidewalk from the hall to the church, I would glance back into what my young eyes saw as the vastness that surrounded the buildings and spread deep into the pitch-black woods from which we were forbidden.

I was not naturally afraid of cemeteries or graveyards. I am the grandchild of a genealogist and some of my fondest memories occurred within these sacred outdoor spaces. They are where I met late family members and heard various accounts of my ancestors, but this was my first forbidden property, so it held a strange power over me.

Those were impressionable years filled with spooky tales and ghost stories. Sitting around a campfire with a multigenerational group of family and friends, I remember our mothers warning our fathers not to frighten us kids with stories of mysterious tombstones with pre-engraved death dates found in attics and creaking sounds in basements that were supposedly empty. Such tales would give us nightmares. I loved listening to those stories while safe within a group of people who loved me, and later I enjoyed retelling these same tales during sleepovers. I've never outgrown my love of reading and sharing spooky tales. Ghost stories encourage togetherness, laughter and, usually, a good life lesson. These stories allow us to discuss history that often is too taboo for general history texts, and they frequently encourage us to look deeper into past stories.

I am an ardent rule-follower, so the graveyard behind Emmaus Baptist Church remained off-limits. It turns out that I would not set foot on the grounds for the next thirty years, although the place frequently showed up in my dreams. Once I returned, I could almost hear our laughter; I remembered where we walked and the very bricks of the building. I remembered where we each stood when we were hanging out and talking. I remembered the games of Red Rover and Freeze Tag. I thought of the three friends who had been there but since passed away. Being there and thinking of them brought them back to life for a moment. The grounds were *haunted* with our memories.

The term *haunted* comes from the Old French word *hanter*, meaning "to frequent," and the Middle English word *haunten* that means "to reside" and it is distantly associated with *home*. Over time, the definition of *haunted* has changed to mean "to make uneasy and restless"; these definitions work for my experiences as a kid. Undoubtedly, many Americans feel a bit uneasy when visiting cemeteries. Their first memories of cemeteries are most likely filled with sadness and mourning. Some even have a deep fear of cemeteries, or coimetrophobia. However, cemeteries were our country's first public parks and have offered visitors places for respite, recreation and research for hundreds of years.

Emmaus Baptist Church, along with over 3,000 properties in Virginia, is listed in the National Register of Historic Places. Virginia cemeteries are popular tourist destinations for their rich histories. They are also popular tourist destinations for their associated ghostlore. Today, the commonwealth ranks at the top of the National Register of Haunted Locations, with nearly 170 spooky sites that claim paranormal activity.[2]

> *Cemeteries are commonly believed to be the most haunted places on earth.... If* [ghosts] *do exist, then surely they must exist in cemeteries.*[3]

Virginians have not always understood haunted places or ghosts to be scary. Reverend Dr. W.A.R. Goodwin, who is given credit for the idea of Colonial Williamsburg and preserving its history, once wrote to a young child, "Shut your eyes and see the gladsome ghosts who once made these places their home. You can learn to call them back....You can train yourself to hear what they have to say."[4] Goodwin did not see ghosts as something to be feared; rather, they were catalysts that could share stories about the past.

In her doctoral dissertation, Alena R. Pirok argues, "Virginians have used ghost stories to identify and make meaning of historical sites....Historical ghost stories sought to highlight the presence of the past, as well as Virginians' close relationship with long-dead historical figures."[5]

Ivor Noël Hume contends, "We might conclude that [Goodwin's] ghosts were the product of his imagination and [had] nothing to do with parapsychology. He simply enjoyed exercising that imagination and used his ghosts as a metaphor for the vicarious pleasures to be derived from walking in the footsteps of history."[6] This resonates with my experience of learning about the rich history connected to Emmaus Baptist Church and my memories from childhood. If only I had found a related ghost story from the past! Pirok reminds me that it is our human nature to tell ghost stories and that new ghosts emerge all the time, so I haven't given up on the possibility.[7]

I began researching to discover the cemeteries across Virginia that are allegedly haunted or have associated ghost stories. Once I had made a list of nearly one hundred, I categorized the cemeteries into regions, since Virginia encompasses over forty-two thousand square miles. I set out on road trips to find the ghosts from the past and learn about Virginia history.

It isn't possible for me to share all their stories, so this is a collection of some of my favorites from over fifty cemeteries across Virginia, along with some "Eerie Extras" that spotlight sensational news items. I have even added some "Spooky Specials" that expand on the related ghost stories from newspapers. Some of the cemeteries that I visited have more than one ghost story.

Many of my favorite Virginia ghost stories related to cemeteries come directly from the pages of newspapers. Some of the ghost stories recount historic tragedies. One news story from 1870 begins by saying there is a "thrilling sensation of a ghost" in a local cemetery.[8] Similarly, with much of the state being touched by war, soldiers from the Civil War are said to haunt the grounds of several cemeteries.

With more presidential burials than any other state, Virginia is known as the mother of presidents, and there are a number of presidential hauntings here. Visitors have heard a whistling president long after his death, and when another president was reinterred, his spirit was left slightly confused about where to haunt.

Not all of Virginia's ghosts are famous. Some are infamous, including Christiansburg's Sunset Cemetery's three sisters in black and the spirits of the 1909 bathtub murder that made headlines across the country, captivating readers' interest in the horrific crime. Each fall, ghost stories of the three sisters can be found in local newspapers, reportedly because of the sisters' fondness for cemeteries when they were alive.

Some of the news stories, including that of a ghost sighting in a cemetery in 1902, share comical tales of what happens when a local takes a shortcut through sacred grounds.[9]

This book includes retellings of newspaper articles, popular regional folklore, local legends and oral histories. I did not create any of these ghostly tales. However, I do share my own experiences from my time visiting cemeteries. There is nothing quite like standing in a place associated with history and hearing ghostly tales, so I invite you to take this book along with you on a tour of the cemeteries of Virginia.

Ghostlore, the traditional beliefs, myths and legends surrounding ghosts and haunted places, connects us to the past and to each other. It helps us preserve local history, traditions and places that might otherwise be lost to time. Throughout my journey through Virginia's cemeteries, the ghost stories shared explore themes of mortality, memory and the unknown.

My storytelling begins in Central Virginia, where I promise you will meet at least one Ghost in the cemetery, and includes tales of United States presidents and their ghostly guests. Among the haunted cemeteries, there is a house built out of marble tombstones from the graves of Union soldiers; from Central Virginia, we'll travel to Northern Virginia and the region to the south and west of our nation's capital, Washington, D.C. Being so close to places connected to our national government, the region holds ghost stories of past presidents and national heroes. I will share tales of Virginia's largest cemetery, Arlington National Cemetery, and a mysterious creature that wailed throughout the night at Mount Vernon. From here, we will travel clockwise around the commonwealth and visit the Tidewater and Coastal Virginia, including Williamsburg, which was the capital of the Virginia Colony from 1699 to 1780 and played a significant role in the American Revolution. This is also the region that includes the oldest known burials in

Virginia. Here, we'll visit a former president's spooky pet cemetery and a colonial graveyard with a monument that has been struck by lightning at least three times! Will you be able to see the famous face in the image that was left behind by this strange weather phenomenon? From here, we will move west to visit the Blue Ridge and Southwest Virginia cemeteries. Here, in the heart of Appalachia, I will share the history of folk art tombstones, and we will visit a cemetery that was established after a mining disaster killed 114 miners. We will even walk part of the Appalachian Trail. I will share stories of sleeping in haunted inns and even overcoming some personal fears. And finally, we'll head north to the Shenandoah Valley and the haunted cemeteries in the western part of the state. One cemetery even lists a "resident ghost" on its website, while another has a ghostly visitor to a grave marker shared by two brothers, both mortally wounded in the Civil War.

While researching this book, I was asked if I believe in these ghost stories. Not all ghost stories are meant to be taken literally, so there are times that I lean into the metaphors of ghosts and hauntings to get to the heart of the tale. Regardless of one's belief in the supernatural, Virginia cemeteries are haunted by the past and hold fascinating stories. Put away your ghost-hunting gadgets and gather round for some good ol' storytelling. But be forewarned, these accounts from history are not for the faint of heart. Prepare to venture into the haunting realm of Virginia's most sacred grounds and uncover the chilling stories from the past.

Part I
Central Virginia

European settlers occupied the land of Central Virginia as early as 1617. This area was touched by both the American Revolutionary War and the Civil War, and where there has been war, visitors will find ghost stories and ghost sightings. The region includes the state capital, Richmond, along with the locations just north and south of the James River.

Our first story comes from the state's capital. The cemetery is one of the most visited in the state for its history and beauty. Hollywood Cemetery is a place that offers numerous legends, such as a spectral dog that protects the graves of children, the Richmond vampire, a crying statue, an alleged witch coven, a ghost that made newspaper headlines in 1870 and the apparition of a former president.

1
HOLLYWOOD CEMETERY

412 SOUTH CHERRY STREET
RICHMOND, VA 23220

Hollywood Cemetery is a 135-acre cemetery in Richmond that was opened in 1849 and constructed on the land known as Harvie's Woods, which was once owned by William Byrd III, the son of the founder of Richmond. The cemetery was designed in the rural garden style, with its name, Holly-Wood, being derived from the holly trees that were found throughout the property.[10] Speaking of trees, this is an excellent segue to share this first spooky tale of an apparition with four paws.

THE BLACK DOG

SECTION C, PLOT 1

Not far from the entrance of the cemetery (enter, turn right and then head up the hill) is a well-known statue, a cast-iron Newfoundland that stands guard over the cradle grave of Florence Bernardin Rees, a little girl who died in 1862. Some versions of the story share that as the sun sets, the statue comes to life and wanders the cemetery grounds, protecting all the little children who are buried in Hollywood Cemetery. Sadly, the black dog has many children to look over, as the child mortality rate at the time of the statue's placement in the cemetery was still quite high, with 34 percent of children not living to their fifth birthdays.[11]

The cast-iron dog statue at Hollywood Cemetery, Richmond. *Author's collection.*

In English folklore, a church grim is a guardian spirit that protects the churchyard, and it is typically depicted as a large black dog with red eyes. The legend is derived from the custom of burying a dog under the cornerstone of a church foundation as a way to create a ghostly guardian. These spectral dogs, which are also called hellhounds, meander cemeteries and crossroads without leaving a trace of their presence.

Richmond's music scene may have added to this folklore and tied it to Hollywood Cemetery. One song, "Howl of the Church Grim," released by The Snake-Handlers in 1985, combined ghostly legends with lyrics that point to the black dog in Hollywood Cemetery having blood on its mouth after the cemetery was vandalized one night.[12] Per the song, the black dog protects more than the little children buried in the cemetery.

Those who have experienced such otherworldly encounters with the dog statue have noticed its eerie eyes watching them as they near the grave. Others have witnessed the statue come to life, only to change positions.[13]

On November 8, 2009, when I was walking in the cemetery on a gorgeous fall afternoon, I, too, saw a black dog at a distance in the cemetery. I had heard of the legend since I was a teen, and because I'm a sleuth at heart, I decided to follow the dog to take a picture with my camera phone. He meandered through the graves and finally stopped by a tree, where he relieved himself before he ran off. At that point, I presumed that the dog was a living creature with biological needs and not a specter. Nevertheless, I tried to keep following him before he completely disappeared. I looked around for a bit before giving up my search.

In 2014, as I was training to become a tour guide for tours of historic cemeteries, I spoke with one of the groundskeepers of Hollywood Cemetery. At some point, the discussion turned to the black dog, and I shared that I had once seen him in the cemetery. The groundskeeper shared that a black dog had lived inside the cemetery grounds for years. With convenient places to hide under mausoleums and among gravestones, access to fresh water and plenty of food left behind by visitors, the dog must have figured that a cemetery might not be such a bad place to be a stray. Whether I actually saw a ghostly pup or the wandering stray remains a mystery—as much as the legend of how the statue came to the cemetery.

One story about how the Newfoundland statue was placed inside the cemetery focuses on how the little girl used to pass by a shop each morning on her way to school. As she walked by, she would pet the statue. When the girl died from scarlet fever, the store owners gifted the statue to the family to serve as a memorial that would guard over the girl's grave.[14] As the girl was not quite three years old when she passed, I have never quite believed that story. Another tale is that the cemetery was a good place to keep the statue from being melted down for ammunition during the Civil War.[15] While it is unclear how the statue arrived in Hollywood, it was forged by The Bartlett Hayward Company, a manufacturer of stoves, and served as the company's mascot in the 1850s, when iron statues of animals were popular lawn decorations.[16] Today, visitors stop by to leave trinkets at the grave and to see the legendary black dog.

Need a bit more ghoul in your ghost story? Let me introduce one of the most notorious residents of the cemetery—the Richmond vampire.

SPOOKY SPECIAL

The cemetery frightened Pulitzer Prize–winning author Ellen Glasgow's dog, Bonnie. Upon Glasgow's passing, she left her estate to her friend and secretary Anne Virginia Bennett. Bonnie was also left in her care. When Bennett visited Glasgow's grave and brought the pup along, Bonnie became distressed and tried to run away.[17]

The grave of author Ellen Glasgow, Hollywood Cemetery, Richmond. *Author's collection.*

Local lore holds that upon Glasgow's death, her last will and testament included a somewhat unusual request. She wanted her late dogs to be exhumed from their graves and then buried with her in her casket in Hollywood Cemetery, an unprecedented request considering pets were not authorized to be buried in a cemetery for humans in Virginia.

Tricia Pearsall wrote, "Ellen Glasgow is entombed with her cherished Sealyham, Jeremy." And in the footnote, she explains, "A telephone conversation with Dan Morris, a former employee of the Frank Bliley Funeral Home, revealed that the funeral workers were requested to unearth the dog's copper casket from the back garden at One West Main. In so doing, they pierced the coffin and had to reseal it before slipping it into the casket with her."[18]

THE RICHMOND VAMPIRE

SECTION D, PLOT 26

When you enter Hollywood Cemetery and stroll toward the river, to your right, you will pass a bunker mausoleum in the Egyptian Revival architecture style inscribed "W.W. Pool 1913." It belongs to William Wortham Pool and his family. This grave is where the Richmond vampire allegedly resides. In the early 1990s, before I became a student at Virginia Commonwealth University, which may be where this story originated, I was told that W.W.

William Wortham Pool's mausoleum, Hollywood Cemetery, Richmond. *Author's collection.*

Pool was a vampire who was allegedly driven from England in the 1800s. To some, the W.W. initials inscribed on the stone resemble double fangs.

In some versions of the story, the vampire is connected to the historic Church Hill tunnel collapse in 1925. Pool was believed to be the bloody creature with jagged teeth who was feeding on victims as they tried to escape the tragic tunnel collapse or the reported creature that left the scene and made its way back to Pool's mausoleum. Most likely, someone saw the railroad fireman Benjamin Mosby, who was working on the steam locomotive when the boiler ruptured after the tunnel collapse. With his body scalded and teeth badly broken, he somehow made his way out of the tunnel. If someone muttered that Mosby was "headed to Hollywood," this was a euphemism during the time that meant he was going to die, which he did.[19]

This is when the vampire story gets a bit weird. Once the bloody creature with jagged teeth was spotted, a group of Richmonders who may have been carrying torches to see inside the collapsed tunnel began pursuing the creature that had made its way from the C&O Church Hill tunnel to Hollywood Cemetery, just under three miles. Once they entered the cemetery, the men saw the creature slip inside the mausoleum. In some versions, this is where the story ends. I have always questioned why these men with torches did not break into the mausoleum to apprehend the creature, but perhaps in 1925, Richmonders were less likely to vandalize cemetery property.

The oldest print version of the Richmond vampire story comes from Garry F. Curtis in April 1976. He was a staff writer for a student paper who describes "the Gothic atmosphere of Hollywood," and within a few paragraphs, he begins to describe the tale's spooky elements.[20] Curtis wrote, "Mr. Poole [*sic*] is alleged to be a vampire. There seems to be a cult in Richmond that has grown up around him....I've heard that it used to be the 'in' thing among medical students to break in and steal parts of his remains. My informant also claims that W.W. was the inspiration for Barnabas Collins on the old Gothic soap opera *Dark Shadows*."[21]

SPOOKY SPECIAL
BONE COLLECTORS AND GRAVE ROBBERS

Leading medical colleges in the nineteenth century needed cadavers for students to learn human anatomy; however, most people felt it sacrilegious to donate a family member's body to a college for study. This need led to college staff stealing corpses from local cemeteries in the dead of night. In Richmond, historic cemeteries traditionally intended for Black residents became the leading targets for this thievery. Chris Baker, a custodian at the Medical College of Virginia, became known as the notorious grave robber who lurked barefoot in local cemeteries, seeking bodies for the school. He also became a boogeyman to local children.[22]

CURTIS FURTHER TELLS THE story of the cast-iron black dog that roams the Hollywood Cemetery at night. And while he may not have believed the story, he wrote, "I have seen what looks like pawprints around the statue." Further, he shares that his guide to the cemetery "mentioned a witch coven centered in Hollywood" that is especially active during Halloween.[23] Curtis does not mention the Church Hill tunnel in his piece. This part of the legend was added in later versions.

A later article in 1993 expands on the rumors of the Richmond vampire, adding that a window in an inner room of the mausoleum had been broken

RICHMOND, VIRGINIA, SATURDAY, AUGUST 1, 1896.

SCENE IN THE DISSECTING ROOM.

The person rolling up his sleeves represents Chris Baker; the other Funeral Director W. S. Selden, and the man partly in the barrel is Solomon Marable. In the rear are the empty benches usually occupied by students when the dissecting of a body is taking place. The Medical College of Virginia, corner of College and Marshall Sts., Richmond, Va., is the place.

The Richmond *(VA)* Planet, *August 1, 1896.*

from the inside.[24] In *Haunted Richmond: The Shadows of Shockoe*, the authors corroborate this story by citing Donald Toney, a longtime employee of Hollywood Cemetery, noting that "the most unusual thing he had ever witnessed in the cemetery was the discovery of a broken glass inside the locked and sealed mausoleum of W.W. Pool." Although their understanding of glass references a broken cup instead of a window.[25]

There are also rumors that "land records signed over the past 100 years, first by Pool, then by others, bear the same handwriting."[26] I have been unable to access such records.

From the records I have accessed, W.W. Pool was born on April 10, 1841, and worked as a bookkeeper, clerk and private secretary. In the 1860s, he moved to Virginia, where he married Alice Cornelia Perdue in 1866,[27] and they had four children. He served as a school superintendent,[28] held a position on the Manchester City School Board in the 1880s[29] and was a Mason[30] and steward of Central Methodist Church, as well as another fraternal lodge.[31] His wife, at about seventy-one years old, passed away on February 6, 1913. W.W. Pool lived until February 26, 1922; he died from pneumonia at the age of seventy-nine.[32] For the most part, nothing about his life raises suspicion.

In 2013, I taught an online course on literary vampires. The class's first short story was Richard Matheson's "No Such Thing as a Vampire," published in 1959. I will not ruin the plot for those who have not read the story, but what appears to be a traditional vampire story is not. To be a bit tongue in cheek, I decided to film my short story introduction in Hollywood Cemetery in front of W.W. Pool's grave to make some parallels between the story and legend. It was July 1. I had not dressed for the hot and humid Virginia summer; rather, I had dressed somewhat elaborately to create a spooky clip for my students. My red lipstick had practically melted, and I was sweating in my black attire as I set up my video camera. The sun felt oppressive. Just as I was ready to push record, thunder clouds rolled in, and within moments, there was a downpour of rain. I quickly grabbed my video

The grave of Samuel Owens in Maury Cemetery, Richmond. *Author's collection.*

camera and tripod, and I ran to my car, hoping not to get too soaked. As soon as I arrived at my car, the rain stopped, and the clouds cleared up as quickly as they had rolled in. I headed back to my spot in front of Mr. Pool's grave. As soon as I set up my equipment, new clouds rolled in, and a line of rain beat down over Hollywood's rolling hills. Was this weird summer weather or a vampire phenomenon? In folklore, just like the Count on *Sesame Street*, vampires can control the weather.

While Pool's life does not resonate with that of a vampire, there is a strange aspect to his story. Pool had been a lifelong friend with a gentleman named Samuel Robert Owens. Both were members of the same Masonic lodge. Pool had been a member for fifty-nine years. Both men were prominent members of the same church and served on the board of stewards. Pool and Owens died on the same day within just a few hours of each other.[33] Their funerals were held on the same day, and their services were conducted by the same church pastor. The interments were in two different locations—Hollywood Cemetery for Mr. Pool and Maury Cemetery for Mr. Owens. While this may be read as a poignant coincidence, it is a bit eerie.

In Mr. Owens's death notice, it reads, "His brain had been paralyzed. Physicians said overwork and no recreation was the cause."[34] Let this be a reminder to all of us to take a break. Might I suggest a stroll through a cemetery, a perfect location for those who enjoy art, history and an atmosphere to contemplate one's choices.

SPOOKY SPECIAL

Ghost of Christmas Past? Dr. Charles Frederick Ernest Minnigerode, the German-born College of William & Mary professor who introduced the German custom of the Christmas tree to Williamsburg, is buried in Hollywood Cemetery in section V, sub-division plot 1. In December, it isn't unusual for visitors to see a small potted evergreen festively decorated with natural ornaments at his grave.

THE HOLLYWOOD GHOST

Spiritualism became popular during the Civil War.[35] Many believed that death was not the end. With a belief that the dead could communicate with

The Hollywood Ghost in Richmond is now a thrillingly sensational subject of conversation in some quarters. There are all sorts of stories current about this apocryphal apparition, which is said to have been seen by divers persons in Hollywood Cemetery within the past two weeks. The police have not yet detected the ghost.

Alexandria *(VA)* Gazette, *June 15, 1870.*

the living, many Americans searched for ways to find comfort and closure while grieving the deaths of their loved ones. Even First Lady Mary Lincoln and President Abraham Lincoln practiced spiritualism and held séances in the White House after the death of their son William.[36] Virginians dealt with their grief in various ways when longing for connections from beyond the grave. To some, this meant seeking mediums and using spirit boards, while others followed more spiritual, religious and familial traditions and visited graves to commune with the dead in metaphorical ways, such as reflecting on memories and sharing stories from the past.

On April 27, 1870, while Virginians were still suffering from the death and destruction of the Civil War and the aftermath of Reconstruction, a mass of spectators gathered at the Virginia State Capitol to hear the verdict by the supreme court of appeals on a divisive case surrounding Richmond's mayoral election. The courtroom gallery gave way and collapsed into the chamber of the house of delegates; 62 people lost their lives and 251 were injured in the catastrophe.[37] Headlines across the nation focused on the disaster and followed news and funeral notices about the victims. Residents and visitors in Richmond shared a collective grief.

Two months after the capital's disaster, news reports about a ghost in Hollywood Cemetery was considered "a thrilling sensational subject of conversation."[38] This was quite a departure from the death notices and tragedy that had headlined the news since the balcony collapse. The Hollywood Cemetery ghost became the talk of the town. For weeks, various individuals witnessed "this apocryphal apparition" within the cemetery grounds, although the ghost continued to elude police, who now served double duty as ghost hunters. The ghost "haunted Hollywood Cemetery" nightly until it was discovered that the spirit was not an apparition but an actual woman in mourning, grieving the loss of her beloved. News reports explain, "The poor creature had dug a hole in the grave of her lover and night after night made her bed there and resisted with all the strength of madness all attempts to remove her."[39] One article offers "a sentimental story of a fair fiancée made desolate by the capitol catastrophe, and who now wanders to where hope and love are buried in his grave, there shedding her ceaseless tears and venting her woful [*sic*] plaints."[40]

The term *ghost* was replaced with labels of "a crazy woman."[41] Cries of sympathy were replaced with orders to arrest the ghost. In mid-August, the woman, who had "excited the fears of the superstitious around Hollywood Cemetery…was arrested" and taken to jail. The woman stated that she was from Rockbridge County, and the reporter lists only her surname—Smith.[42] There were few options at this time for those struggling with grief and mental illness. Asylums were grim, both overcrowded and understaffed. Mental illness was misunderstood, and these asylums offered little in terms of compassionate care. Spotting a ghost in the cemetery had been thrilling news for readers, yet a woman not following a societally accepted approach to grief required law enforcement.

SPOOKY SPECIAL

Built in 1773, The Public Hospital for Persons of Insane and Disordered Minds, which, in 1841, became Eastern Lunatic Asylum and is now called Eastern State Hospital, is a psychiatric hospital in Williamsburg and was the first public facility constructed solely for the care and treatment of the mentally ill. Those interred in the institution's cemetery include thousands of former patients. The graves of the asylum patients who passed away were

Memorial at Eastern State Hospital Cemetery, Williamsburg. *Author's collection.*

Numbered marker at Eastern State Hospital Cemetery, Williamsburg. *Author's collection.*

marked with numbers, not names. In 1986, a memorial was erected that lists the names of those interred in the cemetery.

THE REANIMATED CRYING STATUE

LAWN PLOT 14

Crying or weeping statues are believed to shed tears by supernatural means. Oftentimes, these monuments are associated with religious figures or angels. This isn't the case in Hollywood Cemetery. A marble sculpture of a lady sitting on a tomb and leaning against a cross reportedly comes to life and cries only once a year. The sculpture and grave are listed as belonging to "Colonel Thomas Branch" in *Weird Virginia*, and the authors explain that it "is said to come to life every year on the day of Branch's death and momentarily looks at onlookers with tears in her eyes…then resumes her position until the next year."[43] Yet these details lead to some confusion since the grave marker belongs to John Patterson Branch (1830–1915) and his wife, Mary Louise Merritt Kerr Branch (1840–1896). Their epitaphs are inscribed on the lower sides of the marker. John Patterson Branch was a first lieutenant during the Civil War. His father, Thomas Branch (1802–1888), does not appear to have been in the military, but his grandfather Thomas Branch (1767–1818) was

Branch statue in Hollywood Cemetery, Richmond. *Author's collection.*

the son of Captain Benjamin Branch III of Willow Hill. I'm not sure on which date the statue weeps, so it is difficult to corroborate this claim.

Far more interesting and tragic than this ghostly account is the true story of those who are buried here. John P. Branch sailed to Munich in December 1896, as he was "summoned [due to his wife's] illness." Sadly, travel and correspondence at that time were much slower than they are today. Branch would not find out that his wife had passed until after he arrived in Munich. His wife's death notice was printed in the newspaper while he was at sea without access to the news.

Presidents and Their Ghostly Guests: James Monroe

Section Mount, Plots 1, 2 and 3

Hollywood is currently one of three cemeteries that has two U.S. presidents—James Monroe and John Tyler—buried there.[44] Both presidents are buried in the section referred to as Presidents Circle, and it is in this area that visitors have seen a presidential ghost.

Monroe was a founding father, the fifth president of the United States and the fourth president from Virginia. In 1830, when his wife died, Monroe experienced a deep period of grief and moved to New York to spend his last months of his life with his daughter and son-in-law. Upon his death the next year, Monroe's body was interred in New York City. In 1858, decades after his death, a movement began to bring the remains of United States presidents who had been born in Virginia to a central place within the state. Monroe's body was placed in state in New York on July 3. His body was then placed on board a boat and brought down the Atlantic Seaboard, into the Chesapeake Bay and ultimately up the James River to Richmond on July 4. The reinterment took place the next day. Monroe was buried with full military honors. It was probably one of Richmond's largest spectacles before the Civil War.

Alfred Lybrock was commissioned to design a suitable monument to cover Monroe's remains. In 1859, the Commonwealth of Virginia installed Lybrock's design, "a granite sarcophagus surrounded by a flamboyant Gothic Revival cast iron canopy."[45] Monroe's tomb firmly established Hollywood as one of the foremost places of burial in Virginia. Near Monroe's tomb in Presidents Circle, visitors have seen an apparition sitting in quiet contemplation.[46] Some noticed that the ghost rubs his shoulder. Could this

Above: The grave of President James Monroe, Hollywood Cemetery, Richmond. *Author's collection.*

Right: The grave of President John Tyler, Hollywood Cemetery, Richmond. *Author's collection.*

be a reference to an injury Monroe incurred during the Revolutionary War when he was hit by a musket ball?[47] For some visitors, this might inspire a moment of awe, seeing the specter of a former president; however, I imagine any supernatural encounter in a cemetery can be quite unsettling.

Fearful of seeing two phantom presidents in the same location? Fear not! John Tyler does not appear to haunt Hollywood Cemetery. Instead, you will have to travel east of Richmond to the location where he had wished to be buried. We'll cover that story later in our travels.

2

Monumental Church

1224 East Broad Street
Richmond, VA 23219

Richmond is filled with landmarks associated with tragedy. One of the worst urban disasters occurred on East Broad Street in 1811, and the location held the remains of its victims. The year witnessed many strange occurrences that could make even a skeptic turn superstitious. One newspaper notice reads:

> *In the month of September, a comet made it appearance in the northern part of the heavens, and passing across our hemisphere, disappeared at the south about the end of the year.*
>
> *On the 10th of Sept. the city of Charleston, in South Carolina, was visited by one of the most tremendous hurricanes that ever devastated any country.*
>
> *On the 17th of Sept. the sun suffered an annular and almost total eclipse. The day was remarkable serene, and the skies entirely clear of clouds, so that its appearance was the most solemn and impressive that we could conceive.*
>
> *On the 7th of November, the lives of many valuable Americans were lost in a battle with the Indians* [the Battle of Tippecanoe].
>
> *On the 16th and 17th of December, the western and southern quarters of the United States were alarmed with several shocks of an earthquake.*
>
> *On the 26th of December, the Theatre at Richmond was consumed by fire, and a great number of the most respectable citizens of Virginia perished in the flames.*

Monumental Church, Richmond, Virginia, circa 1903. *William Henry Jackson, photographer; Detroit Publishing Co.; Library of Congress, https://www.loc.gov/item/2016803090/.*

> *In the summer months the heat was, in many places, the most intense that ever was known. In the principal cities several lives were lost by the indiscreet us* [sic] *of cold water.*
>
> *The crops, in many parts of the United States, were destroyed by drought and in many places immense damage was done by overwhelming torrents of rain.*
>
> *These are no common events, and without incurring the charge of superstition, they may be deemed portentous of still greater events.*
>
> *Surely so many extraordinary occurrences, in the course of a few months, ought to excite something of meditation and reflection.*[48]

Days after the December 26, 1811 Richmond Theater fire, committees assembled to count and bury the dead and fundraise for a memorial. The committee responsible for burying the dead determined that the bodies could not be removed from the site of the theater. Although it was not a traditional graveyard, Monumental Church was built on the site where the seventy-six victims lost their lives. Their remains are buried under the church building.

Theatre on Fire.

AWFUL CALAMITY!

A letter from Richmond, Virginia dated Dec. 27, ſays, "Laſt night the theatre took fire and was conſumed, together with about 80 people, with the governor Smith—many were trampled to death under foot, others threw themſelves out of the windows, and were daſhed to pieces on the ground, ſome with legs arms broken. Many were burnt to death in the boxes, and others on the ſtairways."

Later accounts ſay, 160 ſkull bones have been found.

"Theatre on fire. Awful calamity!" A letter from Richmond, Virginia, dated December 27, 1812, says "Last night the theatre took fire and was consumed, together with about 8 people, with the governor Smith many were trampled to death under foot." *Library of Congress, Rare Book and Special Collections Division, Printed Ephemera Collection.*

In folklore, those who die in a particular location are thought to linger there as spirits. Hauntings frequently involve the ghosts of those who experienced tragic deaths or intense emotional experiences at the time of their deaths and who have unresolved business. With so much tragedy in one location, it isn't surprising that church personnel have had unexplained encounters. Some have experienced hearing heavy footsteps when the building was empty. Others say that motion detectors go off when people are not around.[49] Doors open and close without assistance. Even workers' tools seemingly disappear, only to reappear in other locations.[50] While numerous renowned citizens died in this tragedy, reports of hauntings have not identified the spirits rendering the former theater fire location as a collective haunt. A little over one mile away from Monumental Church is a churchyard with a distinguishable ghost.

3

St. John's Episcopal Churchyard

2401 East Broad Street
Richmond, VA 23223

Built in 1741, St. John's is the oldest church in the city of Richmond. There are over 1,300 burial sites with approximately 400 grave markers.[51] St. John's Church is one of America's most significant landmarks. Founding father Patrick Henry gave his famous "Give Me Liberty or Give Me Death!" speech during the Second Virginia Convention at this location. Some of the history connected to those buried in the churchyard is quite haunting; one "angry spirit [roams] the church grounds, laughing maniacally."[52]

Allegedly, the spirit is angry, since, in life, she was mistreated. "Condemnation, a brutal death, and her body being dumped in an unmarked grave were a trio of atrocities"[53] that led the spirit to haunt St. John's Churchyard. To tell this tale, we must travel thirty miles north to Scotchtown to the only original standing home of Patrick Henry, his residence from 1771 to 1778. This was his home when he formed the ideas for his famous speech, and it was from this location that he rode to St. John's Church in Richmond on March 23, 1775, to deliver it.

In 2016, when I first visited the home, my plan was to go to the historic site, which I assumed wouldn't be too incredibly interesting, and then drive to St. John's Church to think about what it would have been like to travel that distance in 1775. Mind you, I would be traveling in a car.

I toured the house with a guide. She noted which portions of the building were reproductions and which were original, including the pine floors. She shared that in the 1930s, the building had been abandoned; it had been

Saint John's Episcopal Churchyard, Richmond. *Author's collection.*

vandalized and lived in by a "squatter" who also brought in wildlife. When the building was restored down to its original paint colors, historians were surprised to find the original doors intact. The hardware was missing, but the wood and all the beautiful craftsmanship were there.

Throughout the tour, my guide pointed to the significant furniture that had once belonged to Henry. One desk she noted was Henry's father's design that he had made in order to better read maps. The underside of the table has a birdcage design, which enables it to swivel in all directions, making map-reading more efficient, as one would only have to move the table instead of the map itself.

She pointed out one of the corner chairs in the room, as Henry died while sitting in one, albeit not this particular chair. She was quick to note that the original is housed in Williamsburg in the Governor's Mansion. She explained that Henry's doctor determined that he was extremely ill. The doctor left him a concoction that was either supposed to heal him or kill him. Because Henry was in such pain, he drank the concoction, which, per our guide, included liquid mercury. Henry died while sitting in a corner chair. When I searched for this information, even using the keyword search "Patrick Henry dies in chair" (I know, I'm that kind of researcher!), I could not confirm this information. Most websites list that Henry died from stomach cancer.

Overall, I thought it was a bit odd to share this with visitors, and by that, I mean that I enjoyed the weird little details. It certainly did not resemble some of the boring tours that I experienced as a young child, when every school field trip seemed to connect to either the Revolutionary War or the American Civil War.

During a good part of the tour, the guide discussed Patrick Henry's relationship with his wife. They had known each other since childhood. Even by the standards of the time, when they married in 1754, they were young; he was eighteen, and Sarah Shelton Henry was sixteen. They moved numerous times. By the time they had had six children and were living in the Scotchtown home in 1771, Sarah was suffering from some kind of serious depression and/or mental illness.

On the "Patrick Henry's Scotchtown" Facebook page, it reads:

> *Shortly following the birth of her sixth child, Sarah Henry developed an antipathy, as they called it, towards her husband and her family. She withdrew from them to the point where she was completely mute and would not feed herself. Her doctor eventually declared her a threat to herself and others. While determining options for his ill wife, there is substantial evidence to suggest that Mr. Henry did visit the Public Hospital in Williamsburg in 1773 but determined that he was not going to subject his wife to such accommodations. Instead, he arranged for her to be cared for at home at Scotchtown, in the basement for the remaining four years of her life.*[54]

Our guide shared details about the Williamsburg hospital, which included barred windows, isolation cells, straitjackets and restraint chairs.[55]

Because there was so little information about mental health in the 1700s, there were few treatment options. Our guide discussed how it was common for those with mental illness to be bled or restrained. Sarah's decline continued during the establishment of the Public Hospital for Persons of Insane and Disordered Minds, now Eastern State Hospital. This hospital was more like a prison, and Patrick Henry did not wish to subject his wife to such treatment. Henry "knew about the hospital and refused to send Sarah there. The Henrys were a family of some wealth, and this probably helped in the decision for Sarah to remain at their home, Scotchtown Plantation."[56]

Further, "Henry's wife, Sarah Shelton Henry, dealt with depression and violent outbursts. Despite recommendations, together they refused to place her in a hospital, instead providing care for her at home until her death."[57] An apartment was created in the home's basement. Sarah always had a nurse by her side, and our guide emphasized several times that she was never left alone.

While standing in the dining room, our guide explained that Sarah's accommodations were directly below us. She asked us to imagine how the family must have felt hearing Sarah screaming below. She also wondered how Sarah might have felt hearing her family dining above. The guide posed good questions that enabled visitors to consider both perspectives.

The guide then asked who was interested in seeing the quarters. She emphasized that there was a great deal of mold and cautioned anyone with any serious allergies. I don't always make the best choices, so I decided to join the group and go to the basement.

Within the basement confines, the windows that had traditionally been wooden have been replaced with glass windows to keep the two rooms sunny. The basement entrance is attached to the exterior of the building. The guide explained that Sarah often complained about feeling chilly in the basement. Even on a somewhat hot and humid day, the area was quite cool.

Included in the quarters was a mannequin wearing a straitjacket dress. Our guide went on to explain that the dress was so small, they had only one intern who was thin enough to try it on. The intern stated that while wearing the straitjacket dress, it was quite calming, similar to a weighted blanket.

Because of Sarah's illness, which, during the time, society believed was caused by demonic possession, she was denied a Christian burial. The guide explained that it is believed that she was buried somewhere on the grounds of Scotchtown. Her grave was not marked with a monument and has not been located.

Two young lovers against the world; one goes mad. This is not a fictional character who is locked away and left alone; it was real life. It appears that Henry and the family visited Sarah as much as they could and as often as she could take the visitations. When I left the building and walked the grounds, I felt sad for many reasons. I wondered, "Where is the body of Sarah Henry?" Some believe her spirit has not gone far.

The ghost of Sarah Henry is reported to haunt Scotchtown. From strange noises, screams from the basement apartment and even staff reporting items being moved when the building was closed to visitors, all signs point to a resident ghost. Witnesses have seen candles lit within the home when no one is there, and visitors have even seen "a woman in a long, white dress emerging from a basement door at the back of the home."[58] Patrick Henry's great-great-great-granddaughter felt Scotchtown was haunted and refused to stay overnight.[59]

Others believe that Sarah Henry is the frightening apparition who haunts St. John's Churchyard.[60] Many notable Virginians are buried there; however, Patrick Henry is not. He is buried in the Henry family cemetery at Red Hill, his final home, in a double box tomb with his second wife, Dorothea Dandridge. Although Sarah reportedly suffered from "diseases of the mind,"[61] scholars argue that it appears she suffered from postpartum psychosis, which was not treatable at the time.[62]

Although I have not seen Sarah Henry's apparition in either location, I am haunted by her story and the treatment of mental illness during that time. Does Sarah Henry haunt St. John's Churchyard, looking for her husband or seeking a proper place to be interred? And is she the quiet apparition wearing a long white dress at Scotchtown? Visit the two historic landmarks, and you may glimpse her ghost.

4

Franklin Street Burying Ground

2009 East Franklin Street
Richmond, VA 23223

The Franklin Street Burying Ground at Twenty-First and Franklin Streets in Richmond was the first Jewish cemetery in Virginia, established in 1791 by K.K. Beth Shalome, the first synagogue in Richmond. The burying ground was filled by 1816.[63] Two of the founders of the synagogue and business partners, Jacob I. Cohen and Isaiah Isaacs, along with their family members are buried in this small cemetery.

Ghost tales haunt every cemetery, even (or especially) buried ones.[64]

In 1840, the City of Richmond raised the grade of Franklin Street by four feet between Twentieth and Twenty-First Streets. The gravestones that were in Franklin Street Burying Ground "were laid flat, and the cemetery was covered with at least four feet of dirt, deeply shrouding all of the grave sites except for the one portion originally reserved for the Isaacs and Cohen families."[65] To protect the family graves, Cohen's descendants enclosed the plot with large rectangular granite blocks. While the family plot was protected, the cemetery was neglected and mostly abandoned until the late nineteenth century. Community members had filled it with debris. There was even a coal yard and a blacksmith shop on the grounds. The cemetery was legally returned to the Jewish community after litigation.[66]

In 1936, local news stories shared some otherworldly occurrences that were witnessed late at night in the cemetery. One resident stated that he saw

Ghosts in Black Walk Through Ancient Cemetery Here

Top: Franklin Street Burying Ground, Richmond. *Author's collection.*

Bottom: The Richmond News Leader, *September 23, 1936.*

two men dressed in long, black robes walk through the locked gates, and "the men, trailing their long black robes, came out of the cemetery and 'sort of sneaked off down the street.'" Locals declared, "The Isaacs and the Cohens are on the loose again!"[67]

Today, the cemetery is surrounded by an apartment building on three sides, with only the cemetery gate exposed to the road. Only two graves in the right rear corner are visible. Although there are records for some of the burials, no complete list exists.[68] While there have been no recent sightings of men in robes or ghosts moving through locked cemetery gates, there are signs of non-spectral activity, including nicely trimmed grass.

5

COLD HARBOR NATIONAL CEMETERY

6038 COLD HARBOR ROAD
MECHANICSVILLE, VA 23111

East of Richmond, there is a national cemetery that comprises 1.4 acres. The United States National Cemetery System includes 164 cemeteries that are maintained by the National Cemetery Administration of the United States Department of Veterans Affairs; the National Park Service, which maintains cemeteries associated with historic sites and battlefields; and the United States Army. The National Cemetery Administration lists a total of 73 Civil War–era national cemeteries that were established between 1861 and 1868.[69]

Established in 1866, Cold Harbor National Cemetery is located on the site of the Battle of Cold Harbor, a two-week action of the Civil War that had devastating casualties.[70] Cold Harbor Battlefield has its share of ghostly activity, including sightings of a mysterious fog, the smell of gunpowder and the sounds of screams, cannons and gunfire.

One reenactor had a disturbing encounter one night under a full moon when he was woken by "the sound of clanking."[71] Because he needed to use the restroom, he set out to identify the sound. He explained:

> *I could then faintly see a campfire, and what seemed to be two reenactors sitting around it. I thought it was odd due to the fact fires aren't allowed on Federal property. I walked closer, I noticed that the two men were talking and were drinking from their tin cups. They were Union soldiers, and had their muskets stacked together, both men were sitting on crates.*

Cold Harbor National Cemetery with the grave keeper's house in the background, Richmond. *Author's collection.*

> *I walked closer and called out....Both men stopped what they were doing, almost like they were frozen in time, they then turned and looked at me....The men were wax-like, white pale skin and their eyes seemed hollow, as if there were no eyes....One of the men stood up and then pointed at me. The other turned and half of his face was shot away, like he'd been hit by a shell and his face exploded! I turned and ran so fast I almost tripped.*[72]

At the cemetery, a little girl who wears a bonnet is said to haunt the grounds. Visitors have seen her peeping out the windows of the gravekeeper's house.[73] Is she related to one of the late veterans, or was she a young guest of the superintendent who has overstayed her welcome? I found no documents of any children being connected to the cemetery. If you're visiting and feel someone watching you, check the windows for a girl in a bonnet staring back at you.

EERIE EXTRA: GHOST IN SEVEN PINES NATIONAL CEMETERY

400 EAST WILLIAMSBURG ROAD
SANDSTON, VA 23150

I grew up nine miles from Seven Pines National Cemetery, which currently comprises 1.9 acres and is surrounded by a brick wall. The cemetery was listed in the National Register of Historic Places in 1995. Like those in other national cemeteries, Seven Pines' markers are placed in orderly rows, the grass is well maintained and the mood is serious. These places reflect the belief that these are hallowed grounds where veterans' sacrifices should be honored.

Growing up in an area surrounded by reminders of war, it was common to hear about ghost sightings of Union and Confederate soldiers still wandering the fields and fighting their battles. Visitors throughout Virginia have reported feeling the presence of these soldiers who lost their lives far from home. Many of the mortally wounded were hastily buried in makeshift graves on the battlefield, and others perished from illness and disease.

Like so many national cemeteries that were nearby or within battlefields, Seven Pines National Cemetery was established in 1866, mostly for interments of the Union soldiers who had been quickly buried without traditional fanfare. The brick-and-stone superintendent's lodge, designed by U.S. Quartermaster General Montgomery Meigs, was built at the southeast corner of the site in 1874. The front of the building is hidden by trees, but when walking up toward the steps to the front door, visitors will notice the tablet engraved with the "Gettysburg Address," which is a distinctive feature of the national cemetery landscape.

The American Civil War was the bloodiest war in our nation's history. Approximately seven hundred thousand soldiers died, more than the number of Americans who died in World War I and World War II combined. A soldier was thirteen times more likely to die in the Civil War than in the Vietnam War.

With hasty burials and the time that had passed, many of the soldiers' remains were not able to be identified. In this cemetery, 1,357 interments are listed as "unknown," which adds to the solemn atmosphere. There are only 150 known dead.[74]

The name of the cemetery is derived from the seven pine trees that were planted along the inside of the cemetery wall in 1869 by the cemetery superintendent; although, according to local lore, the name is derived from the seven pines that were once at the crossroads of Williamsburg Pike and

Seven Pines Has 7 Cedars, 7 Hemlocks! And There's a Ghost in the Graveyard!

Top: The Richmond News Leader, *June 7, 1938.*

Bottom: The grave of John Ghost, Seven Pines National Cemetery, Richmond. *Author's collection.*

Nine Mile Road. Civil War maps include a village with the same name. A 1938 article notes that along with pine trees, there are seven cedars, seven hemlocks and one Ghost.

To tell the story of how a Ghost came to reside in Seven Pines National Cemetery, we must start in Irwin, Pennsylvania, where a couple, Samuel and Mary, had been married for a decade and were welcoming the birth of another child to their family. The year was 1843. President John Tyler was the nation's tenth president, becoming the first vice president to ascend to the presidency after the death of his predecessor, President William Henry Harrison. That year, Edgar Allan Poe's Gothic fiction "The Tell-Tale Heart" and Charles Dickens's ghostly tale *A Christmas Carol* were first published. Samuel and Mary's baby, John, was born into a world that differed from that of the famous writers and politicians who traveled and read widely. John did not attend school but helped his father with farming; and by the age of seventeen, he was listed as a farmer in the 1860 census. The next year, men were being recruited to join the Union army, and John, at the age of eighteen, was mustered into service in Harrisonburg, Pennsylvania, on December 11, 1861.

He served in the 103rd Volunteer Pennsylvania Infantry, Company I, which included 105 men. The infantry advanced on Manassas and were then ordered to the peninsula. The soldiers were involved in a skirmish at Yorktown, the Battle of Williamsburg, a skirmish at Fair-Oaks and the Battle of Fair Oaks, which is also known as the Battle of Seven Pines. Of the 103rd Pennsylvania Infantry Regiment, 3 officers and 50 enlisted men were killed or mortally wounded; 1 officer and 352 enlisted men also died from diseases during the war. Approximately ⅔ of all the deaths of soldiers were caused by infectious diseases, including pneumonia, dysentery, malaria and typhoid fever.

Seven Pines National Cemetery was included in a *Ripley's Believe-It-Or-Not* cartoon because of John's surname—Ghost.[75]

John Ghost died of typhoid fever at White Oak Swamp on June 17, 1862. His remains were moved to Seven Pines National Cemetery, only 1.6 miles from where he died.

Most of the regiment was captured on April 20, 1864. Thirty died in Confederate prisons. Only eleven men remained to be mustered out.

John Ghost was a real person. In fact, his mother, Mary Ghost, filed for a Civil War pension on June 28, 1880, after the deaths of her son and her husband. The family included German immigrants who came to America. With confusion, misunderstanding and illiteracy, surnames were frequently misspelled. John Ghost's ancestor Kraffgoss became Kraft Ghost. Today, descendants use the last name Coast.

When you enter the cemetery, immediately walk to the left. Under the shade of a tree, you will find Private John Ghost's grave in section B, site 156.

The cemetery is open daily from sunrise to sunset. It's best not to disturb the dead after hours![76]

SPOOKY SPECIAL

Need help finding a grave in a national cemetery? Each national cemetery includes a gravesite locator stand with a listing of the individuals who are

The back of Ghost's grave shows the grave number. *Author's collection.*

interred in the cemetery, along with their corresponding gravesite numbers that are engraved on the back of each marker. In larger cemeteries, such as Arlington National Cemetery, the gravesite number will start with the cemetery section number.[77]

6

Randolph, Wight and Ball/Thompson Family Cemeteries

12601 River Road
Richmond, VA 23238

Just thirteen miles west of Richmond is Historic Tuckahoe, located in both Goochland and Henrico Counties. The first portion of the house was built in 1733 by William Randolph. A young Thomas Jefferson, whose father had been friends with Randolph, spent seven years of his youth, from ages two to nine, here.[78] It was here that he learned to read and write. Today, visitors can see several original outbuildings and the schoolhouse. The grounds include the Randolph, Wight and Ball/Thompson family cemeteries, and there is also a resident ghost.

When walking the "Ghost Walk," a walkway lined by trees, it isn't hard to imagine seeing a shadowy presence as the path limits one's sight, almost like a hedge maze. The Ghost Walk is the traditional name for the path from the main house to the cemetery, and it is here that there have been sightings of the gray lady.

Gray ladies are often said to be ghosts of women who died for lost or unrequited love. They are described as those who are still pining for their lost loves, and many of these spirits are those of women who died violently.[79]

The apparition at Historic Tuckahoe has been sighted walking down the path, lingering near the cemeteries and moving within the house. Some visitors have seen the gray lady dressed in what appears as a wedding gown, while others have only heard her sobs. During one sighting of the gray lady inside the house, a shadowy form went through a closed closet door. The

The ghost walk leads visitors to the Randolph, Wight and Ball/Thompson family cemeteries, Richmond. *Author's collection.*

guide, who witnessed the ghostly visitor, felt a chill throughout her body and needed some time to gather herself before continuing her work.[80]

The gray lady has been well documented at Tuckahoe. In the early 1990s, a guest took a photo that captured the image of the gray lady; however, over the years, her image has faded from the photo, making it difficult to see the once-clear features that identified her as having blond hair and blue eyes and wearing a bonnet.[81]

There are theories about who she might have been when she was alive. Some call her the "unhappy bride," referring to Mary Randolph, who was one of "[Thomas] Jefferson's orphaned second cousins…[and] grandmother of John Marshall, fourth Chief Justice of the United States."[82] Mary was in love with an overseer, and her parents forbid her from pursuing the relationship. She ran off to be married but was forcibly brought home and made to marry someone else. She later went insane.[83]

Another theory is that the gray lady is the ghost of Thomas Randolph's second wife, Gabriella, who was much younger than her husband and not beloved by his children from his first marriage.

Randolph, Wight and Ball/Thompson family cemeteries, Richmond. *Author's collection.*

The third and most compelling theory is that the gray lady is Judith Randolph, who is buried in the cemetery on the property. Judith married her cousin Richard Randolph of the Bizarre Plantation. The couple had children, including John St. George Randolph.[84] Their marriage became complicated when accusations were made about Richard killing an infant, one his mistress had given birth to. To make matters worse, Richard was believed to have been having an affair with Judith's sister Ann, who went by her nickname, Nancy. Richard was accused of murdering Nancy's baby to hide the affair and the illegitimate child. This became a scandal that went to court, with John Marshall and Patrick Henry serving as two of the defense counsels. Randolph was acquitted, and Nancy and he did not have to go through a trial. Judith's revenge may have been murdering her husband, Richard, by poisoning him. This did not stop her from going insane.[85] Their son St. George, who was deaf, was adopted after his father's death by his uncle Senator John Randolph from Virginia, a friend of future President James Monroe. Monroe made arrangements for the teen's schooling and escorted him abroad.[86]

The Randolph family was considered quite superstitious, as their outer doors were "cross and Bible doors," which blocked evil spirits from passing through, and their porch ceilings were painted in the traditional haint blue.[87] Gray ladies take their name from their frequent appearance as women dressed in gray or their manifestations in shades of gray.[88]

SPOOKY SPECIAL

Gray ladies are ghosts in amorphous forms, meaning that they lack a clear shape and structure. With blurred and indistinct boundaries, gray ladies have been described as appearing like a mist or smoke. They do not necessarily dress in the color gray; instead, the image of the apparition from the corner of one's eye often appears gray.[89]

ON NOVEMBER 23, 2023, I visited Historic Tuckahoe while wearing a gray dress. I figured that even if I didn't see the gray lady, I should at least make a nod to her existence. I took the self-guided tour that is available on the site's website. While walking the grounds, a young boy who must have lived on the property nearly ran into me as he was playing with some peers. He saw me, and before running the other direction, I hope that he mistook me for the gray lady—at least for a moment.

A somewhat uncanny event occurred after I left Historic Tuckahoe. I stopped at Greenwood Memorial Gardens in Goochland to visit the graves of my maternal relatives and a friend. The flat headstones are flush with the ground, and I always think that my friend's grave is located closer to the road than it is. While I was looking for her grave among the other flat bronze grave markers, I noticed that leaves were covering one grave. I could see just enough of it to notice that it was a veteran's marker, so I carefully swept off the leaves with my boot. As I was gently moving the leaves aside, a large black puff of smoke billowed into the crisp autumn air. It turns out that while I was clearing debris from the grave marker, puffballs, a type of mushroom that erupts on contact, lurked under the leaves. Had I thought to snap a photo, it would have made a great addition to this book, as the black smoke-like substance lingered in the air like a ghostly apparition. While visitors are not likely to make contact with ghostly fungi, the more frightening creatures in the cemetery are the Canada geese that can be territorial and aggressive. Give them a wide berth, and you will need to worry only about ghosts following you home.

A good amount of our time has been focused on historic ghost sightings in and around Richmond. After visiting Jefferson's childhood home, it seems fitting for us to move west to Albemarle County, where Jefferson was born and later made his home. I promise, we're heading there. First, we need to travel south to Petersburg, formerly a trading post called Peter's Point, named after Peter Jones, who commanded Fort Henry and traded with the American Native tribes in that region. In 1733, William Byrd II, who founded Richmond, envisioned a city there, which was renamed Petersburg.

7

BLANDFORD CEMETERY

111 ROCHELLE LANE
PETERSBURG, VA 23803

Blandford is a 189-acre burial ground, making it the second-largest cemetery in Virginia, with Arlington National Cemetery being the largest. The cemetery has been used as a burial ground since the early eighteenth century, with its oldest grave dated 1702.[90]

The cemetery has a long history connecting it to both the Revolutionary War and the Civil War. One of its burials is that of Major General William Phillips, the commander of the British troops during the April 25, 1781 Battle of Petersburg. Phillips led one of the British army's most successful campaigns in the American Revolution. When he died of a fever on May 13, 1781, his body was brought to Blandford Church Cemetery, where it was buried in a secret location.[91]

The Memorial Day holiday is believed to have been inspired by events that occurred at Blandford Church Cemetery. After the Civil War, schoolgirls began placing flowers on the graves of soldiers, a tradition that was repeated annually.[92] In June 1866, Nora Fontaine Maury Davidson instituted the first Memorial Day observance in Petersburg at Blandford Cemetery.[93]

There is a mass grave for 30,000 soldiers, of which the records only include 3,700 names, located on Memorial Hill.[94]

With drops in temperatures, even on the hottest days, and sightings of apparitions of soldiers wandering among the old tombstones, Blandford is believed to be one of the spookiest and most haunted cemeteries in Virginia.[95]

Blandford Cemetery, Petersburg. *Author's collection.*

One haunting tale that continues to be told merges the past and present. Francis Antomatti (1821–1844), a man who was well known throughout the town, was a native of Corsica. He was deeply in love with a local woman who did not share similar emotions. In his hopelessness, he came to the church on July 31, 1844, where he "went to the gallery window of the church and gazed at the sun fast sinking behind the house where lived his false sweetheart."[96] The church was abandoned at the time, and as the sun set, he took his own life. In the cemetery, his headstone reads, "Honour was his only vice." The tablet is a replacement for the original that was destroyed by vandals. In 1964, restoration efforts by the Cockade City Garden Club had the inscription re-lettered.[97]

In 1998, an article in the newspaper shared the events of one of Blandford Cemetery's tours that included luminary candles being placed throughout the evening tour to help visitors negotiate their way. With rainy weather, many of the luminaries were snuffed, except for Antomatti's candle, which continued to burn despite the showers. The site coordinator for the event noted the uncanniness of this candle and added, "Perhaps his ghost is still unsettled."[98]

Another haunted tale often shared is that of Major William H. Jarvis (1824–1877). Although his marker has been weathered, making it hard to read, it notes that he was chief engineer of the Petersburg Fire Department for many years. The story that is shared says that Jarvis was placed in a glass-topped coffin, and his grave was not covered with dirt so that when his wife visited him in the cemetery, she could see him. In time, she remarried and had a thick marble slab added to cover the tomb. Major Jarvis did not seem interested in having his grave covered. Reports began to emerge that the slab had been pushed out of place. Allegedly, no matter how many times cemetery workers slid the heavy stone back into place, it would always be found ajar the next time they returned. Author M. Clifford Harrison explained, "Once, when walking with a friend at Blandford, I mentioned the legend of the hollow tomb. We walked to the Jarvis Square and paused outside the iron fence. Suddenly, we heard a loud metallic clink down in the grave."[99] At this point, they believed the story had been confirmed.

On June 14, 2022, I was startled not by a ghost or a loud metallic sound but by a baby deer that still had its spots. It wandered into a fenced family plot to munch on some foliage when we saw each other. He tried to squeeze himself through the fence, which was not possible. I moved away so he wouldn't hurt himself or the fence.

EERIE EXTRA: COFFINS WITH WINDOWS

Patented in 1848 by Almond Dunbar Fisk and manufactured in Providence, Rhode Island, the Fisk metallic burial case was a cast-iron coffin popular in the mid-nineteenth century among wealthier families. The airtight case was custom formed to the body, with sculpted arms and a glass window plate for viewing the face of the deceased. From an advertisement in 1851, "[These] will be sought for by those who cherish the noble sentiment of protecting and preserving the human remains of their deceased friends against the desecration of the grave."[100] John C. Calhoun (1782–1850), who served as the vice president under John Quincy Adams and Andrew Jackson, was one of the first to popularize the iron coffin. It was particularly useful during the Civil War, when Calhoun's body needed to be moved to deter desecration by Union soldiers.

SARCOPHAGUS OR METALLIC BURIAL CASES.—Having the exclusive agency for the city of Richmond to furnish Fisk's & Raymond's Metallic Burial Cases, the subscriber informs his friends and the public generally, both in town and country, that in addition to his usual assortment of different kinds of wood Coffins, he is prepared to furnish any size of the patent Metallic Burial Cases, which presents to the public every valuable quality for an article of this character, either for deposit in the earth or in vaults, or for the purpose of preserving human remains from decomposition, when necessary, with a view to their transportation to a distance.

The Metallic Burial Case will be sought for by those who cherish the noble sentiment of protecting and preserving the human remains of their deceased friends against the desecration of the grave. Testimonials may be referred to from the most distinguished men of the country who have witnessed the utility of these patent Metallic Burial Cases. Persons wishing to see them will call on me at the store of Mr. Wm. Booth, No. 140 West Main street, or at my coffin wareroom, in the rear of the agricultural store of Mr. H. Baldwin No. 148.

mh 12—1aw4w JOHN TURPIN.

Advertisement. *From the* Richmond Daily Times, *March 22, 1851.*

8

Poplar Grove National Cemetery

8005 Vaughan Road
Petersburg, VA 23805

In 2016, I attended a hard hat tour of Poplar Grove National Cemetery. I love seeing rehabilitation efforts that are in progress at cemeteries. The tour was a behind-the-scenes look at the rehabilitation project at Poplar Grove National Cemetery. During the Siege of Petersburg, Union soldiers who were killed in battle were hastily buried near where the battles took place. This land had been the campsite for the Fiftieth New York Volunteer Engineers. During the war, they constructed a Gothic Revival pine-log church called Poplar Grove. When looking for a location for a national cemetery, this seemed like a good place. When the bodies were disinterred from their hastily buried plots, many were difficult to identify. After all, the headstones, if there were any, had been made of wood. For this cemetery's macabre tale, we must travel three miles down the road to the notorious "tombstone house."

Tombstone House

Located at 1736 Youngs Road, the house was built in the 1930s after the superintendent of Poplar Grove National Cemetery decided to reduce lawn maintenance costs by turning upright grave markers into flat markers. This required cutting off the bottoms of each marker and placing only the top portions flat on the ground. The 2,220 bottom portions of the markers were sold to a gentleman who proceeded to build his dream house out of the

The "Tombstone House" in Petersburg. *Author's collection.*

materials. One legend purports that the markers were fully removed, and the names that were inscribed on them were turned inward when the home was constructed, hiding them from outside eyes. Some believe that the stones are too large to have been made only from the bottom portions of the markers.

Since some believe that desecration was involved in the home's construction, the property is considered haunted. Perhaps this was the making of a haunted house or simply upcycling in a poor economy. When I drove by, I didn't notice that it was creepy; instead, I thought that it was beautifully landscaped.

That controversial decision to use grave markers in the home's construction could not be repeated today. The United States government requires that all grave markers that are removed from a national cemetery be destroyed to the point that they cannot be recognized.

Our next stop is located in Charlottesville, known colloquially as C'ville.

9

Maplewood Cemetery

425 Maple Street
Charlottesville, VA 22902

Maplewood Cemetery is a city-owned cemetery that was established in 1827, although its oldest known grave marker dates to 1777.[101] The cemetery is located a few blocks from downtown Charlottesville and 1.5 miles east of the University of Virginia, which was founded in 1819 by Thomas Jefferson. Although the cemetery is relatively small, there are hundreds of burials there, both marked and unmarked, with most burials dating to the Civil War. Maplewood Cemetery is unique for including the remains of enslaved Africans, Civil War soldiers and Freemasons side by side in 3.6 acres.[102] With such a diverse range of burials, it is no surprise that the hauntings are just as varied. From disembodied sounds, strange chills and sensations to manifestations, visitors have noted the unnerving stillness in the cemetery. Some report "feeling the sensation of a mysterious, cold phantom caressing their arms and faces," along with "ominous noises…including whispers and quiet sobs."[103]

One perpetual mourner is referred to as the woman in white, based on her flowing white attire. Legends about women in white or white ladies are found around the world. These spirits are associated with local legends, including accidental deaths, murders or deaths by suicide, along with themes of loss, betrayal and unrequited love. While it doesn't appear that Maplewood's spirit has been identified, some locals have captured her image. The apparition appears in photos as a misty figure.[104]

Maplewood Cemetery is just under thirteen miles from one of Albemarle's most famous hauntings, the Moon Ghost of Albemarle, which filled newspapers around the state in the late 1860s.

EERIE EXTRA: MOON GHOST OF ALBEMARLE

> The Scottsville Register *of November 11, 1867 carried a long account of the ghost which seems to have been based on an interview. It sold like "War Specials" in Richmond....Reprints were made and still Lynchburg and other places clamored for more.*[105]

Lawyer John Schuyler Moon secured a summer property in southern Albemarle County known as Church Hill, "a small two-story frame structure with about eight or nine rooms, a one-story wing, and two porches. The front porch, which was about four steps from the ground and without a roof, was directly beneath the window of the upper hall. There were many oddly shaped closets, one of which had an entrance from the roof of the wing [that was] later known as the 'Ghost Closet.'"[106] The house was situated between two cemeteries, which one might consider a quiet family getaway; however, from August 1866 to 1868, the Moon Ghost, or "Jake Ghost," visited the family frequently. The ghost created what the family called "the ghost eye" and would "make a light travel around the room 'at the height of a man's eyes,' even when the blinds were closed and extra bed covers hung over the curtains."[107] In the candlelight, "a small light no larger than a quarter of a dollar [was] played upon the walls of his house, sometimes a much larger spot, then a narrow streak. Sometimes a flash and sometimes a broad glare."[108] The ghost took their groceries, including coffee, sugar, flour, salt and meal, from the home and poured molasses over the concoction; then it dumped this "'witches brew' and a family Bible on the roof, a favorite spot with him."[109] The ghost was not only a nuisance, but it would also throw rocks and dinner plates from the roof. It wore chains that could be

ANOTHER MOON GHOST.—One muddy night, during Christmas week, while we were in the country, mysterious noises were heard over the house—doors opening, hollow sounds inside the walls, hoarse voices in the yard, strange growling, and, above all, the ringing of the back-door bell, which had not been heard for years. At intervals, all night long, this bell was heard. The sleep of the household was broken, and many were the speculations, at the breakfast table next morning, as to the cause of these queer noises, especially the bell-ringing. It could not have been the wind, because there had been much windier nights, and the bell had never stirred. Just as we had reached the conclusion that the Moon ghost had emigrated from Albemarle, a young gentleman, who had gone to examine into the matter, returned and reported that the old black hen had selected the transom, close by the bell, as a lodging place for the night. *Hinc Mae lachrymae!*

Not another "moon ghost" but an old black hen! *From* The Native Virginian, *January 3, 1868.*

heard rattling as it moved around the roof and escaped when bullets were fired at it.[110]

During one incident, Moon and his teen son waited up one night to try to catch the troublesome ghoul. Around midnight, Moon's son spotted a ghostly figure climbing up the back porch to the roof and entering the home through the "ghost closet."[111] The Moon Ghost used this closet to slip in and out of the house, typically unnoticed.

The frequent news articles about the ghost led "thirty or forty" University of Virginia students to trek from campus to the Moon residence.

> *Some of them were bragging quite a bit about what they could do as they were not afraid. Grandpa mentioned the fact that he always put the bravest one in the graveyard to watch, and the bragging immediately ceased.*[112]

Moon hired detectives to investigate the disturbances for two weeks, but nothing occurred in their presence. Finally, after years of torment, the ghost left a note "written in pencil on cheap paper with a zig-zag scrawl," explaining that it would no longer "pester" the Moon family, and the mysterious occurrences stopped.[113]

Dr. Frances Moon Butts explained that her uncle had prosecuted a horse thief gang leader named Lucien Beard. From the penitentiary in Richmond, Beard sent a letter to Moon offering "to explain the Moon Ghost if [Moon] would secure his pardon [but] the letter went unanswered, and the Moon Ghost has never been explained."[114] Dr. Butts noted, "The Moon Ghost bears evidence of the unsettled conditions of that crucial reconstruction period…when a president was assassinated, [and] Jefferson Davis was ransomed from a cell at Fortress Monroe."[115]

The Moon Ghost may have haunted more than just one Moon family household. Reports said that the Moon family "had had a like visitation at an old Moon estate in England."[116]

Although there are no tours of the property the Moon Ghost of Albemarle once haunted, today, visitors have several options for tours of Maplewood Cemetery, including tours given through the Albemarle Charlottesville Historical Society and US Ghost Adventures. Of course, because Maplewood Cemetery is located within a walled property, those who wish to spy its woman in white can simply hang around outside the wall on a moonlit night in the hopes of catching a glimpse.

10

UNIVERSITY OF VIRGINIA CEMETERY

CEMETERY ROAD
CHARLOTTESVILLE, VA 22903

The University of Virginia Cemetery was founded in 1828 and serves as the final resting place for prominent individuals associated with the university and its students. One student interment that made headlines was that of John A. Glover of Alabama, who was tragically murdered in 1846. While Glover and his peers were attending the exhibition of Raymond & Co.'s Menagerie of Animals, he tossed a burning cigar in the arena, which spooked a lion and caused havoc. The enraged trainer struck the student with a large tent peg, which caused the twenty-one-year-old's death.[117] In a tribute of respect, university students wore black armbands for a month.[118]

One Virginia alum, Confederate General Carnot Posey, was wounded in the thigh at the Battle of Bristoe Station on October 14, 1863. After a month of battling infection, he died and was interred in the University of Virginia Cemetery. The story of his death is shared during tours of the cemetery, especially with students who reside in the lawn room 33 West. This is where Posey once lived as a law student, and it is the very room in which he died. Don't be afraid to visit his grave! Posey's ghost spends its time haunting the residents of his former room, 33 West.[119]

> *The reverence for the deceased was sometimes set aside for ghoulish matters. Like other medical schools during the 1800s, anatomy instructors at UVa faced a dilemma. Laws at the time prohibited the dissection or possession of human cadavers....Drastic measures sometimes were taken* [including] *nocturnal visits to the UVa cemetery for the purpose of digging up recently interred corpses.*[120]

University of Virginia Cemetery, Charlottesville. *Author's collection.*

Along with its tragic stories, like other universities with medical schools, the University of Virginia has a dark history of grave robbing. However, community members did not passively allow their loved ones' remains to be taken. They fought back.

> *Grave robbing at the UVa cemetery became common enough that people started taking measures to defeat the perpetrators. A favorite ruse was to hold a mock burial during the day and bury a log or bundle of rocks wrapped in a shroud. The real body would then be brought to the cemetery during the hours of darkness and buried in secret.*[121]

Heading down Alderman Road late at night? You may want to bypass Cemetery Road, where visitors need to only be traveling near the cemetery for an eerie experience. Reports include vehicles being engulfed in a peculiar mistiness. At a distance, the mist resembles a bluish-gray coloration that lends to the spooky atmosphere of the old cemetery. This dense mist or fog even dampens sounds, which makes the environment seem eerily quiet. This is an especially odd occurrence considering the road is so close to student dormitories.

11
MONTICELLO GRAVEYARD

1050 MONTICELLO LOOP
CHARLOTTESVILLE, VA 22902

Just five miles east of Maplewood Cemetery is the property of Thomas Jefferson, a founding father, the author of the Declaration of Independence, the third president of the United States and the second president from Virginia. While Jefferson called Monticello "his essay in architecture," its name means "little mountain" in old Italian. He inherited the property from his father, Peter Jefferson. This is where Thomas Jefferson lived, where he designed his own gravestone and epitaph and where he was laid to rest.

When two friends die on the same day in different locations, it is a bit eerie. Remember the story I shared of W.W. Pool, who is buried in Hollywood Cemetery, and his close friend Samuel Robert Owens dying within hours of one another? That seems strange, yet Thomas Jefferson's death was the ultimate uncanny event, because it occurred on the same day that the second president of the United States, John Adams, passed. Even more unnerving, they both died on Independence Day exactly fifty years after the signing of the Declaration of Independence—July 4, 1826. They lived, breathed and died preserving their belief in our country's great experiment.

Wanting to preserve his legacy, and with March 1826 believed to be when he signed his final will, Jefferson designed his own gravestone and prepared the text that was to be engraved on it. The epitaph reads, "Here was buried Thomas Jefferson / Author of the Declaration of American Independence / of the Statute of Virginia for religious freedom / & Father of the University of Virginia."

Thomas Jefferson's tombstone, University of Missouri Campus, Columbia, Boone County, Missouri. *John A. Bryan, historian; Lester Jones, photographer; Historic American Buildings Survey; Library of Congress, https://www.loc.gov/item/mo0312/.*

Today, when you visit Monticello and the Jefferson Family Cemetery, you will not see Jefferson's original obelisk but a replica. Because visitors continued to chip off parts of his gravestone for personal souvenirs, the grave marker and marble epitaph that were originally erected at Monticello in 1826 were donated by his descendants to the University of Missouri in 1883.[122] The replica marker includes Jefferson's birth and death dates, with "Born April 2, 1741 O.S." signifying old style of recording dates; it means that Jefferson was born when the Julian calendar was used, which is behind the Gregorian calendar. Now, we celebrate Jefferson's birthday on April 13.[123]

Before heading to Monticello on May 26, 2024, I stopped at The Thomas Jefferson Center for Historic Plants, which "collects, preserves, and distributes historic and native plant varieties and strives to promote greater appreciation for the origins and evolution of garden plants."[124] That Saturday, the center was holding one of its open house events, where there are lectures and plant sales. The nursery is located at Jefferson's Tufton Farm, land that was passed down by his father. The nursery has a few notable collections, including "China, Gallica, Musk, Moss, Damask, and other once-blooming, antique and species roses."[125] Many of these roses at the center are directly linked to those Thomas Jefferson planted. Experiencing this rose garden feels like a deeply personal way to connect with history. The fragrance of the flowers is much like a specter—it appears and then vanishes. Both are hard to describe and even harder to capture. History is not so different. It is complex and often inequitable. The deeper we dig, the more skeletons we discover. On this recent trip to Monticello, before I even purchased a grounds ticket, I first visited The Burial Ground for Enslaved People.

BURIAL GROUND FOR ENSLAVED PEOPLE

The Burial Ground for Enslaved People holds the remains of more than forty people, although there are no formal headstones; this sacred space honors the more than four hundred enslaved people who lived and labored at Monticello during Jefferson's lifetime. The burial ground enables descendants of Monticello's enslaved community a space to pay respect to their ancestors.

Researching ghost stories before arriving and learning that they have not been able to identify those who are buried here, I was surprised to hear no ghostly tales of the enslaved Africans of Monticello. As historian Tiya Miles explained, "Tours of supposedly haunted places are a booming business. In the South, these tours often take visitors to homes where slaves died at the hands of their masters or cemeteries where slaves are supposedly buried…

Burial Ground for Enslaved People at Monticello. *Author's collection.*

and exploit the very real suffering that took place in the Antebellum South."[126] Today, Monticello does not shy away from its dark past or the story of Sally Hemings. The site's online exhibit calls her "daughter, mother, sister, aunt. Inherited as property. Seamstress. World traveler. Enslaved woman. Concubine. Negotiator. Liberator. Mystery."[127] Sally Hemings is "one of the most famous—and least known—African American women in U.S. history." It is hard to understand why she returned to Virginia with Jefferson's family after traveling to France, where she was free.

I stood in a place where unknown individuals who were enslaved at Monticello rested while thinking of the Hemings family, although Sally Hemings does not rest here. Her final resting place is unknown, although historian Cinder Stanton believes she "may be on a parcel of land near the University of Virginia Medical School. The lot was sold to [her] sons, after they were freed upon Jefferson's death, and [she] was…living with them in a house on the property. She is thought to have been buried behind the house, somewhere on the acre her sons owned."[128]

I reflected on which graves are marked and which are left unmarked—and even how graves are marked. While many of us now believe memorials for the dead are important, past Virginians did not share the same opinion. These decisions were based on money, family preference and what was fashionable at the time.

> *Ghost stories, after all, are one of the ways we talk about historic injustices and crimes unavenged...while ignoring the cruelty and horror of chattel slavery is one of many ways the past gets whitewashed. The ghosts of slavery are still here, though sometimes they don't lurk in creepy old buildings. Sometimes they are right in front of your face.*[129]

PRESIDENTS AND THEIR GHOSTLY GUESTS: THOMAS JEFFERSON

I purchased a grounds ticket and walked from the visitor's center up to the Monticello Graveyard. Monticello was crowded, as it was Memorial Day weekend, but many visitors took the shuttle bus directly to the house or the graveyard. The walk was pleasant and shaded by trees, which is a bonus during hot days. I thought about how Jefferson had walked this property and may have taken these same steps I was treading. I considered the complex history of this place. The trail was a haunting reminder about how one can easily get turned around in the woods, which also made me think of Jefferson's love of geography and maps, a love he inherited from his father, who surveyed the land. I am of the generation who spent their childhoods playing in the woods, so not being able to see anything but trees can be fun and unnerving, especially because Monticello is also a place with an otherworldly presence, including "mysterious footsteps and other sounds."[130] There have been several reported ghostly encounters inside the home as well as on the grounds. After the site closes to visitors and twilight overtakes the land, distinct sounds of humming and whistling, sounds Jefferson was known to make when he lived, have been reported.[131] As I walked, I listened closely for whistling, which would have been easily drowned out by the songs of spring birds.

After a fifteen-minute walk, I arrived at the cemetery, which includes over 270 memorials surrounded by an iron fence. Jefferson's memorial, this second obelisk that was paid for by Congress and erected in 1883, is made of granite and is close to the fence, making it easy for visitors to view without being able to touch it. Before this, in 1836, the original marker was moved closer to the house to protect it, just three years after the stone had been erected.[132] Tangible history and souvenirs were just as important in the

Thomas Jefferson's grave at Monticello Graveyard. *Author's collection.*

nineteenth century as they are today; a similar statement can be made of grave vandalism. Just as visitors wished to take a part of Jefferson's legacy with them, for decades, visitors have left coins at Jefferson's grave.[133] Today, members of the military leave coins at graves in order for the deceased soldier's family to know that someone has visited the grave.

SPOOKY SPECIAL

In Greek mythology, the ferryman of Hades, Charon, required payment for his services. This led mourners to leave coins with their loved ones' remains to ensure their passage across the River Styx and into the world of the dead. Souls who could not pay were forced to wander the world of the living and haunt those they left behind for at least one hundred years.

SIGNAGE NEAR JEFFERSON'S GRAVE reads, "The graveyard had its beginning in an agreement between two young men, Thomas Jefferson and Dabney Carr, who were school-mates and friends. They agreed that they would be buried under a great oak which stood here." The sign shares information about the first burial, "Carr, who married Jefferson's sister, died in 1773. His was the first grave on the site, which Jefferson laid out as a family burying ground. Jefferson was buried here in 1826."[134]

During my visit, the graveyard was visited by many families, and I noticed how young boys tried to squeeze themselves through the iron gate. My favorite ghostly tale of this cemetery is how one young boy who was bored with his parents meandering Jefferson's gardens made his way down to the cemetery and pressed his way through the fence. Perhaps the sweat he had built up from running around in the garden helped him slide through the tight space. He looked around at the old grave markers and Jefferson's obelisk. After some time had passed and clearly worrying that he might get in trouble for wandering off, he attempted to exit the cemetery through the same iron bars—only this time, he was stuck inside. He called for help to no avail. Eventually, he was met by a gentleman in period attire who calmly sat down on one of the graves and began chatting with the young boy. The boy must have thought a Monticello worker had taken pity on him. Regardless, the chatting calmed the boy's nerves enough that he was no longer frightened. He talked with the gentleman openly, and the older gentleman assured the boy that his mother would soon arrive. Sure enough, he could hear his mother calling his name, and then he saw her running toward the cemetery. The boy turned to the gentleman, perhaps for advice so that he wouldn't get in too much trouble or simply to point out his mother. As he turned, he noticed that the gentleman in period attire had completely vanished. The boy looked around, and there were no living souls inside that cemetery except for himself.[135] Was the ghostly gentleman who eased the mischievous boy's mind the phantom of our third president? Visit the cemetery one evening before closing, and listen carefully for whistling.

12
MONTPELIER

11350 CONSTITUTION HIGHWAY
MONTPELIER STATION, VA 22957

With Madison's Montpelier thirty miles north of Monticello, I decided to visit the graves of James and Dolley Madison the same day I visited Jefferson's. James Madison, another founding father who served as the fourth president of the United States from 1809 to 1817, was acclaimed as the "father of the Constitution" for his pivotal role in drafting and promoting the Constitution of the United States and the Bill of Rights. Madison's personality has been described as quiet and introspective, so while a spectral figure resembling him has been seen sitting and thinking, it is Dolley Madison's ghost that is more frequently seen.[136] And it is Dolley Madison's son's "wrathful ghost" that has made headlines. Montpelier docents shared that Payne Todd, Dolley Madison's son and James Madison's stepson, behaves poltergeist-like if anyone dares to speak poorly about him or his exploits while in his bedroom in the house. One docent had been cautioned but ignored the warning. After she told visitors about how Payne lost everything that had been left to his mother by Madison—to the point that Dolley Madison became impoverished—and that Payne "gambled, drank, womanized and went to jail a few times," she immediately felt the consequences. She had a sharp pain in her leg that blistered almost immediately after she spoke ill of Payne and even got into a car accident on her way home from Montpelier. The incidents escalated until another docent encouraged her to apologize to Payne's ghost.[137] She did and no longer felt his fury.

James Madison's family cemetery at Montpelier. *Author's collection.*

An even stranger tale comes from ghost author L.B. Taylor Jr., who shares stories about the "albino beasts of Montpelier." In one instance, a couple saw a ghostly polar bear walking the grounds, while another couple shared that the creature appeared while they were riding horses and looked like a snow-white animal "calf."[138]

While these haunting tales are fascinating, I'm much more interested in the family cemetery and seeing the maker's mark on their gravestones. The maker's mark, a distinctive feature that includes the maker's initials or full name, can be found on some gravestones and is an indication of who created the gravestone. One particular mark connected me to home, as the marker was carved by John W. Davies, a Richmond sculptor who had close ties to Hollywood Cemetery. This interests me partially because I like learning about gravestone makers; it also reminds me that Madison's grave was unmarked for twenty years, following a family tradition. There were no gravestones in the Madison family cemetery until the mid-nineteenth century, which parallels the changes of society's practice of commemorating the dead.

The Madison family cemetery is a short walk from the Montpelier visitor center. The cemetery is surrounded by a brick wall. Visitors can enter the cemetery through an iron gate with the name "Madison 1720." A large magnolia stands outside the brick wall on the right side of the cemetery, where James Madison's and Dolley Madison's obelisks are located. The obelisks are kept behind a chained partition to discourage visitors from being too close to touch the memorials. There are several family markers throughout the family cemetery, along with a few trees.

After Madison's death in 1836, John Quincy Adams, the sixth president of the United States from 1825 to 1829, delivered a passionate oration celebrating Madison's role in the formation of our government. After her passing in 1849, Dolley Madison's will included a request for a simple marker for her husband's grave.[139] Madison's obelisk was added only after Hollywood Cemetery hoped to acquire and reinter the remains of the Virginia presidents: Jefferson, Madison and Monroe.[140] When preparing a memorial, Madison's coffin had to be disturbed to set a proper foundation. During the process, bystanders could not help but gaze upon the late president's body.

> *In digging for a suitable foundation, it became necessary to go below the coffin, which was consequently exposed to view. The boards placed above the coffin had decayed, but no earth had fallen in upon it, and everything appeared to be as when the coffin was deposited there, except that the coffin-lid was slightly out of place, allowing a partial view of the interior. As there were no fastenings to prevent, the part of the lid covering the superior portion of the body was raised, and the several gentleman present looked in upon the remains of the great Virginian.*[141]

Having a grave disturbed would certainly be grounds for an apparition to haunt the premises, but again, it is Madison's wife's ghost that is more often seen.[142]

PRESIDENTS AND THEIR GHOSTLY GUESTS: JAMES MADISON

In life, Dolley Madison was viewed as one of the livelier first ladies, despite her Quaker upbringing and the anguish she must have felt after losing her first husband, a son and her in-laws to yellow fever. In her second marriage, she was energetic and outgoing, and she served as an excellent hostess, even throwing the first Inaugural Ball on her husband's inauguration night. Her legacy lives on in Virginia and in Washington, D.C., especially in the famous

Rose Garden at the White House, which is credited to Dolley Madison. Dolley Madison's legacy is not all that lives on. Many believe that she divides her time, making ghostly appearances at Montpelier, the White House and at the Cutts-Madison House, where she lived in her final years.[143]

If ghosts linger at a property where they have unfinished business, Dolley would certainly spend a good amount of time at Montpelier. Madison's health declined in the 1830s. Immediately before his death, his niece, who was keeping him company, asked if there was something the matter. Madison replied, "Nothing more than a change of mind, my dear." And then he passed in his bedroom on June 28, 1836.[144] He was eighty-five years old.

After Madison's death, Dolley Madison moved to Washington, D.C., where she later passed. She was not originally buried in the family cemetery beside her husband; instead, she was reinterred in 1858, after first being buried in Congressional Cemetery in Washington, D.C.[145] Perhaps not being able to rest peacefully together or having their graves disturbed explains the hauntings.

SACRED SPACE: MONTPELIER BURIAL GROUND OF THE ENSLAVED

During my visit, I walked from the Madison family cemetery to the Montpelier Burial Ground of the Enslaved, which was undergoing an archaeological survey and closed off to visitors. Numerous flags in a variety of colors could be seen as part of the survey; they were used to "define the boundaries for this sacred site so [they] can protect and honor the ancestors buried here," according to the signs surrounding the site.

One grave that is not located here is that of Paul Jennings, the enslaved personal servant to James Madison who became an antislavery activist and author. Jennings's book *A Colored Man's Reminiscences of James Madison* was published in 1865 and is considered the first memoir about life at the White House. Jennings died in northwest Washington, D.C., in 1874 and was buried at the Columbian Harmony Cemetery, a cemetery for Black individuals that was located at Ninth Street Northeast and Rhode Island Avenue Northeast. The cemetery was closed in 1959, and Jennings's remains were reinterred in a mass relocation to National Harmony Memorial Park in Landover, Maryland.[146]

THE OMINOUS END

With Civil War spirits, a gray lady at Jefferson's childhood home and a pondering president just feet from his second grave, the ghosts of Central Virginia could spook the unspookable. There are plenty more haunting stories to uncover here, but the ghosts from other regions of the commonwealth are summoning us. Let's travel to our next tour stop, Northern Virginia, where we could meet the apparition of our nation's first president along with the ghosts who haunt Virginia's largest national cemetery.

Part II
Northern Virginia

Northern Virginia, colloquially known as NOVA, includes the region just west and south of our nation's capital. In 1673, Thomas Lord Culpeper was given a charter and later named royal governor of Virginia, although it took him years to visit the region. Today's visitors will find colonial and Civil War–era memorials and museums, along with the headquarters of the U.S. Department of Defense, the Pentagon and the headquarters for the CIA. NOVA also includes Virginia's largest cemetery, Arlington National Cemetery, which is one of our spooky stops on the tour of this region. Traveling north from Central Virginia, our first stop is the oldest churchyard in Fredericksburg.

13

St. George's Graveyard

905 Princess Anne Street
Fredericksburg, VA 22401

Located on Princess Anne Street, this cemetery was established in the early 1700s, with "the first legible date [as] 1752," although there were burials here long before this time.[147] St. George's Graveyard includes a variety of styles of gravestones, including tablestones, obelisks, ledgers, shouldered tablets, etc. Today, visitors can see the third church that was built in 1849, which replaced the rebuilt church from 1815.[148] One of the more famous burials is that of Colonel John Dandridge, the father-in-law of George Washington.

I love self-guided tours. They offer flexible scheduling and let visitors travel at their own pace, which is beneficial for ghost tours. On January 2, 2024, I took the Ghosts of Fredericksburg tour through the Action Tour Guide app, which includes over fifteen tour stops, including St. George's Episcopal Church Cemetery, also called St. George's Graveyard.

I started the tour a bit after 8:00 p.m. January is a cold, dark month; Victorians believed telling ghost stories was the perfect way to pass a winter evening. I couldn't agree more. St. George's was one of my last stops, which only increased the suspense. While I did not enter the cemetery grounds, the graveyard can be seen from the street by looking through the iron gate. Honestly, that was close enough, considering the reports of unexplained mists and orbs being spotted in the graveyard, especially at night.

The ghost tour shared that a caretaker of the cemetery once felt someone touch him, only to not find another living soul in the cemetery. Along with this disembodied touching, Fredericksburg police continue to have odd

St. George's Graveyard, Fredericksburg. *Author's collection.*

encounters with the churchyard—both in and outside the church. Even dogs trained for K-9 police units show their nervousness in the cemetery and near the entrance of the church.

In Marguerite DuPont Lee's *Virginia Ghosts*, she recounts the story of a young lady named Ella McCarty, who sang in the choir of St. George's. On one evening, she arrived early and was alone except for her companion and the organist. The church was quite dim, and Ella was left alone while the organist and her escort went to find lamps. As Ella sat quietly, she noticed that she was not quite alone—a woman dressed in white with a veil over her face was kneeling in the church. She watched the woman rise, turn to face her with a sad expression and suddenly vanish.[149]

While I try to focus exclusively on ghosts *in* graveyards, I include this story, as the event took place in 1858 in the third church building. Because it was larger than the prior buildings, it required "some graves and the unknown bodies [to be] all reinterred under the basement floor."[150]

For a closer look at those interred in the graveyard, the styles of the graves and even their typography, St. George's offers several self-guided tours on its website.[151]

14

Aquia Episcopal Church Cemetery

2938 Jefferson Davis Highway
Stafford, VA 22554

Traveling just thirteen spooky miles north of Fredericksburg, our tour takes us to Aquia Church Cemetery. Here is the oldest church in Stafford and the childhood church of George Mason, known for his authorship of the Virginia Bill of Rights and Constitution. The church's historic sign shares that the communion silver had to be buried during three wars in 1776 (the Revolution), 1812 (the War of 1812) and 1861 (the Civil War). The churchyard is one of the oldest in Stafford that is still in use. The first recorded burial occurred in 1838, but with many family cemeteries being moved to Aquia, the oldest tombstone dates to 1698. The cemetery includes many styles of markers, including tablestones, treestones, obelisks and crosses.

Spooky Special

The use of memento mori in the United States began with Puritan immigrants, who brought both their familiarity with the frailty of human life and their aversion to unnecessary embellishment to North America. The iconic skull, with or without crossed bones, fit the Puritans' aesthetic nicely and can be seen in seventeenth-century graveyards throughout New England and the upper Mid-Atlantic.

This stark, plain imagery can occasionally be seen in early seventeenth-century funerary markers in Virginia, although it is uncommon and appears to be confined to high-status gravesites.[152]

Aquia Episcopal Church Cemetery, Stafford. *Author's collection.*

The skull on the grave of Christian Brown Graham, Aquia Episcopal Church Cemetery. *Author's collection.*

Some of my favorite grave markers in this churchyard include Reverend Alexander Scott's (1686–1738) angel and crest; his wife Sarah Scott's (1692–1733) tablestone with angels and a skull and crossbones design; and Christian Brown Graham's (1719–1742) grave that includes the memento mori skull and crossbones. While I was visiting in the middle of the day, no one else was around. In such a cemetery, with old funerary artwork, it might be easy to let one's imagination wander. As the sun dips behind the trees, tombstones might trick one's brain into thinking they are not alone. Of course, only authorized personnel, including cemetery caretakers, are allowed on these sacred grounds at night. Cemetery management spend a great deal of time in the cemetery and have become accustomed to noticing the slightest changes in grave markers. Their experiences with eerie tales do not help ease anyone's fears. For example, one former caretaker at Aquia Church Cemetery recalled seeing white, blurry shapes among the tombstones.

In Marguerite DuPont Lee's *Virginia Ghosts*, she recounts the story of William Fitzhugh, who reminisced about the Civil War. He recalled that he and another soldier had had a hard day while on a scouting mission and decided to get some rest by lying on the church pews, "notwithstanding they knew the church was considered haunted." While they were resting, they heard footsteps near the rear of the church. Then they heard someone whistling the tune "The Campbells Are Coming." As the soldiers looked for the person who alerted them, they discovered no one else in the room. As they glanced out the door, they saw a battalion of soldiers coming straight for the church. The resting soldiers leaped out of a window and escaped capture. They "always attributed their escape to the whistling of the ghost."[153]

Virginia Ghosts also includes a story about "a lady of independent fortune and social position" who was interested in the hauntings of Aquia and set out to investigate the church. Unable to find any brave volunteers to stay the night with her, she hired two scientists to record any sounds they heard. As she led the scientists into the church, she felt a hand slap her in the face with such force that the mark remained for days. With the commotion of trying to apprehend the disembodied hand, they were unable to record any of the noises that night.

Finally, DuPont Lee shares the story of the apparition looking out a window, which apparently belonged to a woman who had been murdered and whose skeletal remains had been placed within the church. On a dare, one man, who declared he was not at all frightened, entered the church at night and was given a hammer and nail so he could show proof the next day that he had entered the church and its belfry. His peers waited for him outside in the churchyard while he entered the sanctuary. After an hour, the man had not returned. The group investigated and discovered that the man had hammered the nail as he had planned, but the nail had gone through his coat. The group surmised that as he tried to leave, the man must have felt something tugging on his coat, holding him back. Perhaps assuming someone had grabbed him, the man died of fright after he accidentally nailed his own coat to the wall in the belfry.[154]

As we leave Stafford County, we will travel thirty miles north to the historic home of George and Martha Washington.

15
Mount Vernon

3200 Mount Vernon Memorial Highway
Mount Vernon, VA 22121

Here at the home of General George Washington, founding father, commander of the Continental army in the Revolutionary War and the first president of the United States, you'll find the mansion, his gardens, two tombs and a burial ground of the enslaved who lived, worked and died here.

Mostly, all that I learned about George Washington in my youth was mythology. His teeth were not made of wood; instead, they were a collection of teeth from other humans and animals. He did not wear a white wig but instead kept his hair long and powdered it, which was popular during the time. *Washington Crossing the Delaware*, the 1851 painting by German artist Emanuel Leutze, depicts a bold and regal General Washington directing his compatriots through the frozen river on their way to victory at Trenton. Washington was forty-four years old, and this action was a gamble with popular support as the war waned.[155] With all the myths about George Washington, it isn't a surprise that ghost stories about him go back to 1806, just seven years after the president's death.

Mount Vernon is 115 miles north of my childhood home in New Kent County, the home of Martha Dandridge, who married Washington. My best friend's backyard practically bordered St. Peter's Churchyard. The church, built in 1703, was designated "the first church of the first First Lady," and it was the first churchyard that I frequented. In January 1759, the rector of St. Peter's Church joined Colonel George Washington and Martha Custis

The tomb of President George Washington, Mount Vernon. *Author's collection.*

in marriage. If I'm being honest, I really wanted to find Martha's ghost, although it appears that it is George Washington's ghost that greets guests.

Washington died at Mount Vernon on December 14, 1799. His will expressed his wishes to be buried at Mount Vernon, and knowing that the family tomb was deteriorating, he left funds for a new brick tomb to be constructed after his death. Upon his death, he was buried in the old tomb. In 1831, after the completion of the new tomb, George and Martha Washington's bodies, along with those of other family members, were moved out of the old tomb. The old tomb remains on the grounds for visitors to view.

The Washington tomb has attracted many famous visitors, but I cannot help but reflect on poet Emily Dickinson's visit in 1855, when she was twenty-four years old, because it differs so much from my own recent visit. In a letter, Dickinson wrote, "One soft spring day we glided down the Potomac in a painted boat, and jumped upon the shore—how hand in hand we stole along up a tangled pathway 'til we reached the tomb of General George Washington, how we paused beside it, and no one spoke a word."[156] I also visited Mount Vernon on a spring day—Wednesday, May 29, 2024—in the afternoon right before a thunderstorm, which made the visit a bit more hospitable considering there were nearly a dozen chartered buses parked in front of Mount Vernon. As soon as I entered, I realized that the place was practically overrun with a middle school's field trip. I first walked to the new tomb, which was crowded. Visitors stood in line to be able to walk up and peep in the tomb. The place was anything but quiet.

Numerous ghostly sights and sounds have been reported, along with a few unwanted brushes with the other side. Reports include disembodied sounds, like singing, along with visitors being touched by the skirts of apparitions who do not appear. Other phenomena include alarms being triggered when no one is around and fluctuating temperatures.

During my visit, a thunderstorm that had not been on my weather app brought a downpour. It was a welcome surprise for me. I was standing by the old tomb that is east of the new tomb and closer to the Potomac River. The school visitors crowded each location that I visited on the grounds. With the school group students screaming that they were melting from the rain, a tree near the old tomb kept me practically dry.

I walked to the burial ground of the enslaved, which includes a monument that was dedicated in 1983. This burial ground includes the grave sites of

The original family tomb of George Washington, Mount Vernon. *Author's collection.*

both freed and enslaved Black Americans who worked at Mount Vernon from the 1750s into the nineteenth century, including Washington's personal servant William "Billy" Lee, who was granted his freedom and an annuity in Washington's will. Lee was also granted the option to remain at Mount Vernon, which he chose to do. Lee's brother Frank, who served as a butler, and Frank's wife, Lucy, who served as a cook, were among the enslaved at Mount Vernon, along with their three children, Mike, Philip and Patty. Although Lee does not have an individual marker, a visitor to the cemetery in 1846 described seeing the grave "of Washington's favorite servant, who was with him in his campaigns, fulfilling his simple duties faithfully and affectionately. The spot is not forgotten, though the tramp of passing years has leveled the little mound."[157]

In my research, there was only one presidential home that included the ghost story of an enslaved person—that of William Lee.

BURIAL GROUNDS OF THE ENSLAVED

The Slave Memorial & Cemetery, as it is listed on the visitor's map, is on the southernmost end of the property near the Potomac River. The cemetery is located in a wooded area that is completely out of view, except for the path that leads visitors to the monument. It is here, on the edge of the woods, walking among the trees, that visitors have reported seeing the apparition of William Lee.[158]

The burial ground and memorial to the enslaved, Mount Vernon. *Author's collection.*

Lee served as Washington's valet throughout the Revolutionary War. After the war, Lee continued his work, traveling with Washington. In one incident, while Lee was carrying a chain for Washington, he fell and broke his kneecap. He continued to accompany Washington on his travels, although Lee later broke his other knee, which required a steel base to heal. Afterward, Lee was reassigned to make shoes, since he needed a job he could do while seated.[159] While there are not many details about the sighting of Lee's ghost, I wonder if his injured knees held a clue to the apparition's identity.

Presidents and Their Ghostly Guests: George Washington

One of the first stories of a presidential haunting comes from 1881. Josiah Quincy recollected his father's ghost story from Mount Vernon. His father was Josiah Quincy III, a prominent politician who served in the U.S. House of Representatives. When visiting Mount Vernon to meet with George Washington's nephew Bushrod Washington, Quincy III experienced more than a casual meeting. As an overnight guest, Quincy III was offered and accepted Washington's bedchamber, which had reportedly been haunted by the late president. Quincy III had his own ghostly sighting of Washington that night.[160] I cannot imagine how Quincy III or anyone staying overnight in Washington's bedchamber, where the president passed, could recall details of a ghostly visit, especially when sleeping in a poster bed with drapery that resembles that from a classic ghost story like Sir Walter Scott's "The Tapestried Chamber" (1828). Quincy III shared his story with family members and said he suspected that Washington lingered near his grave due to relic-hunters, who continually disturbed the tomb, and those visitors who continually touched his possessions. Of course, others believe that Washington haunts his tomb simply because he loved this land, his home.

Spooky Wails Haunt Mount Vernon

"Spooky Wails Haunt Mount Vernon," The Daily Progress *(Charlottesville, VA), May 18, 1979.*

WASHINGTON'S GHOST, BIGFOOT OR A PEACOCK?

Strange sounds of "wailing and screaming nightly" could be heard for "nine noisy months" in 1979. Nicknamed the Mount Vernon Monster, the creature was believed by some to be a sasquatch, while others believed it was "hoot owls, loud frogs, a radio with a stuck button, wild boars, a prankster with a bullhorn, the ghost of George Washington, the ghost of George Washington's pigs" or a peacock. Experts from the nearby wildlife refuge noted the peacock could have been a peafowl, which are kept as yard pets, and they hypothesized, "One could have flown the coop and fluttered to Mount Vernon."[161]

Leaving the eerie noises and possible monsters behind, we travel just over nine miles north to Alexandria, a city on the Potomac River known for its brick sidewalks and well-preserved eighteenth- and nineteenth-century buildings. This is where founding fathers dined. Today, King Street is lined with boutiques, bookstores and specialty shops. Just a few blocks away is the area known as the Wilkes Street Cemetery Complex, which includes thirteen cemeteries. The Alexandria Common Council decreed that graves were not to be dug within the limits of Alexandria after 1804 due to concerns of disease. Alexandria churches purchased land on the corner of Wilkes and Payne Streets, an area that was once Spring Garden Farm. Today, the oldest tombstone that can still be read was erected in Christ Church in 1771. The cemetery in the complex that seems to draw the most visitors includes a ghost and an interesting—albeit odd—love story.

16
SAINT PAUL'S CEMETERY

601 HAMILTON LANE
ALEXANDRIA, VA 22314

In March 1895, the neighborhood near Saint Paul's Churchyard witnessed quite a fright. Reports circulated of an apparition that resembled a tall woman "attired in white [that] glided from an alley and would vanish before any one [*sic*] could get close enough to make an investigation."[162] The ghostly figure knocked on one local woman's door. She answered and then "slammed the door to and ran back in the house." A storekeeper "summoned courage to approach [the ghost] and asked what he could do for it." He received no reply. When a police officer who did not believe in the supernatural arrived, the apparition turned out "to be a well-known resident of the neighborhood, who, for amusement, was masquerading."[163] One might wonder why a community would readily accept this figure was a ghost instead of assuming it was human prank, but Saint Paul's Cemetery has a long history of haunting and mysterious visitors.

The cemetery located in the Wilkes Street Cemetery Complex is haunted by the ghost of the female stranger who is buried there. As the story is told, in 1816, a mysterious woman who was sick for three weeks died at Gadsby's Tavern across the street from the cemetery. The man with her, believed to be her husband, made everyone around them swear that they would never reveal their identity. The epitaph on her tablestone tomb reads, "To the memory of a female stranger whose mortal sufferings terminated on the 14th day of October 1816. Aged 23 years and 8 months. This stone is placed here by her disconsolate Husband in whose arms she sighed out her latest breath, and who under God did his utmost even to soothe the cold dead ear

"The Grave of the Female Stranger" at Saint Paul's Cemetery, Alexandria. *Author's collection.*

of death." This engraving appears with verses from Alexander Pope's poem "Elegy to the Memory of an Unfortunate Lady." The tombstone was quick and pricey, and the husband paid for it, although his payment bounced, and he promptly left town.

While little is known about the female stranger and her partner, numerous theories say that she was Theodosia, the daughter of Aaron Burr, founding father and third vice president of the United States; she disappeared in 1813. Unlike many fathers of the time, Burr believed that his daughter should have the same education as a man. During her life, Theodosia was known for her education. It is believed that she was either lost at sea, murdered by pirates or shipwrecked in a storm.

Today, St. Paul's Cemetery preserves the story of the female stranger, while many haunting reports of a young woman dressed in nineteenth-century clothing have been made in the cemetery and in Gadsby's Tavern.

I love a good mystery. I went to visit the grave of the female stranger in St. Paul's Cemetery in July 2021. I visited the entire complex of thirteen cemeteries over approximately eighty acres. Visiting the grave today hardly requires a guide. Enter "the grave of the female stranger" in Google Maps, and you'll be taken directly to the table grave.

While you're visiting, be sure to visit the graves of Aida and Minna Simms, who are better known as Ada and Minna Everleigh or the Everleigh sisters, notorious American madams. They operated a high-priced brothel known as the Everleigh Club in Chicago that was open from 1899 to 1911.[164]

From here, we'll move east toward the Potomac River to take a ghost and graveyard tour!

17

Old Presbyterian Meeting House

323 South Fairfax Street
Alexandria, VA 22314

On October 29, 2023, I had a book signing at Old Town Books in Alexandria. It was this town's Family Trick or Treat Day, and the streets were filled with kids and families in costumes. We had had such nice fall weather during the prior month, but on that day, I was reminded that Virginia summers often have one final heatwave. The temperature was in the mid-eighties, and it was sunny. Many of the kids and family members in costumes looked like they were going to melt. One father was dressed in a polar bear costume, and I hoped he had an icepack tucked somewhere in his suit.

I thought it would be a fun day to check out the trick or treaters, and after the book signing, I wanted to walk around town and take Alexandria's Colonial Tours' Alexandria's Original Ghost & Graveyard Tour. I booked tickets for 7:30 p.m., which left the perfect amount of time between my book signing, some shopping and a dinner at a local restaurant, which served pumpkin spice margaritas.

While on the tour, we went through an alley and down some streets in the area to hear ghostly tales and some pretty good/bad dad jokes. There was a bit of history, some questionable history when it came to a story about a burial and the biggest disappointment about the ghost and graveyard tour—it didn't include any graves or graveyards!

Before I scream "false advertising," there were two routes, a northern and southern route, and the weekend before Halloween isn't the best time to take a tour. The tour guides were probably exhausted from packed

Old Presbyterian Meeting House Churchyard, Alexandria. *Author's collection.*

schedules, and the streets are crowded with activity. Because "graveyard" was in the title of the tour, I pulled out my Find a Grave app and found the nearest churchyard—Alexandria's Historic Old Presbyterian Meeting House and Churchyard. I headed over and realized that this was the churchyard where the Tomb of the Unknown Solider of the American Revolution is located. In 1826, the body of an unidentified man wearing a Revolutionary War uniform was unearthed and reinterred in the current boundary of the meetinghouse's burial ground. Flowers were placed on his grave annually, and the memorial that we see today was dedicated in 1929. The epitaph reads:

> *Here lies a soldier of the Revolution whose identity is known but to God. His was an idealism that recognized a Supreme Being, that planted religious liberty on our shores, that overthrew despotism, that established a people's government, that wrote a Constitution setting metes and bounds of delegated authority, that fixed a standard of value upon men above gold and lifted high the torch of civil liberty along the pathway of mankind. In ourselves his soul exists as part of ours, his memory's mansion.*

Normally, I would not have entered a churchyard at night. I was hesitant about doing so until I realized that the church was filled with a congregation watching a silent movie. The gates were open, and the churchyard was well-lit. Plus, there was a large sign to remind visitors that everyone is welcome.

The visitor's guide brochure shares that the churchyard was active as a burial ground between 1760 to 1809 and includes the remains of over three hundred people, including "Andrew Wales, the first commercial brewer in the Washington area"; a confidant of George Washington, Dr. James Craik; Thomas Porter, "who participated in the Boston Tea Party"; as well as an unidentified Revolutionary War soldier, "whose remains were unearthed just to the north of its current tomb" and was reburied in this churchyard in 1826.

I had a fun book signing event in the cutest bookstore, had a great dinner, saw some amazing home decorations, had great guests on my tour and found a graveyard with haunting history!

18
Arlington National Cemetery

1 Memorial Avenue
Arlington, VA 22211

Arlington National Cemetery is a 639-acre military cemetery in Arlington across the Potomac River from Washington, D.C. Before the land became a cemetery, it was a 1,100-acre plantation where 63 people of African descent were enslaved. It was the home of George Washington Parke Custis, whose father was the stepson of George Washington and who was raised at Mount Vernon. When George Washington Parke Custis passed, the property was left to one of his daughters, Mary Anna Randolph Custis, who married Robert E. Lee, a future Confederate general. Once the Civil War began, the family left the house, and it was confiscated through a tax auction.

Prior to the Civil War, most American soldiers were buried in churchyards or family cemeteries. As the United States' population grew, cemeteries were moved out of city centers into more rural areas. The first of these rural cemeteries, which were designed like parks, was Mount Auburn in Cambridge, Massachusetts, dedicated in 1831. The first garden cemetery in Virginia was Hollywood Cemetery, which opened in 1849.

As the death toll rose from the numerous battles of the Civil War, there was a great need for a national cemetery in the area to accommodate more soldier burials. Established in 1864, Arlington National Cemetery is the country's largest military cemetery and serves as the final resting place for more than four hundred thousand military veterans. Arlington is currently one of three cemeteries that holds the remains of two U.S. presidents; Presidents William Howard Taft and John F. Kennedy are buried here.

With its dark history and proximity to battles, Arlington National Cemetery has a reputation of being haunted. One place with paranormal activity appears to be the Fort Myer Old Post Chapel, which is technically outside of the cemetery, and the Fort Myer gate that enters Arlington National Cemetery on Meigs Avenue on the western side of the cemetery. The chapel has been used by the cemetery since the 1930s for worship services and weddings, and it is the last place family members are able to grieve over their loved ones as they lie in repose. With so much emotional turmoil fixed on one place, one would expect the chapel to be haunted. What is unexpected is that active-duty service members have reported disembodied voices and footsteps and even sightings of a grief-stricken ghostly woman. While military personnel have their share of superstitions, they are also trained to remain confidential and arguably stoic. Military dogs, part of K-9 units, have refused to enter the chapel at night, even when locked doors have become unlocked.[165] It's best to keep your distance from that entrance. Fortunately, the visitor's center is on the eastern side of the cemetery. But that isn't the only place a visitor might see a ghost!

TOMB OF THE UNKNOWN SOLDIER

Perhaps the most iconic memorial in the cemetery is the Tomb of the Unknown Soldier, which is a neoclassical, white marble sarcophagus with Washington, D.C., as its backdrop. This is the final resting place for one of America's unidentified World War I service members and unknown dead from later wars. This is a place of mourning and reflection. It is not a place one might expect to see a ghost.

Soldiers from the Third U.S. Infantry Regiment, or "The Old Guard," stand watch over the tomb twenty-four hours a day every day of the year in all weather conditions. Depending on the month, the ceremony known as "the changing of the guard" occurs every hour or half hour. The sentinels of the Tomb of the Unknown Soldier are considered elite members of the Old Guard. During the ceremony, visitors are instructed to stand and remain quiet.

An infantry soldier who was stationed to the Old Guard at Fort Myer shared some ghostly tales from tomb guides. In 2008, there were sightings of a lady in a red dress who wanders the cemetery, presumably searching for her lost love. The lady's attire is not merely the common patriotic attire

Tomb of the Unknown Soldier, Arlington National Cemetery. *Author's collection.*

of visitors; it is described as a ballroom gown that appears to be from the nineteenth century.[166]

Another apparition is heard but not seen. People often recognize that Arlington National Cemetery has a funeral caisson, a horse-drawn cart that was originally used to transport ammunition during military battles and the wounded or dead from the battlefield. Tomb guards have shared that they heard the caisson and the clopping hooves of horses. Although the use of the horses that carried the caisson was paused in 2023 due to the well-being of the animals, the unusual part of the tomb guards hearing the caisson in 2008 was that the soldiers heard the sounds at night, when funerals do not take place.[167]

Another frightening report says that soldiers have repeatedly heard screams coming from a particular mausoleum near the tomb's amphitheater. Along with these sounds, some soldiers have witnessed an accompanying eerie green light.

PRESIDENTS AND THEIR GHOSTLY GUESTS: WILLIAM HOWARD TAFT

William Howard Taft, the twenty-seventh president of the United States, served from 1909 to 1913. After leaving the presidency, he served as the tenth chief justice of the United States from 1921 to 1930 and is the only person to have held both offices.

> *The Taft administration evidently held an unusual attraction for the "other side." For it was during this regime that employees began reporting daily sightings of their first woman ghost—Abigail Adams, wife of the second President. The First Lady in the White House was known to have used the East Room to string out the family wash. Servants in the Taft era claimed to see Abigail walking at daybreak right through the closed doors of the East Room, her arms outstretched.*[168]

The haunting of the former first lady was not the only ghostly sighting. There was the "Thing," a teenage male ghost. In a letter from Taft's military aide Major Archibald Butt to his sister Clara, he wrote, "It seems that the White House is haunted....The ghost, it seems, is a young boy....They say that the first knowledge one has of the presence of the Thing is a slight pressure on the shoulder, as of someone were leaning over your shoulder."[169] While Major Butt and his sister may have enjoyed the staff's gossip, President Taft did not. When Butt shared stories of the "Thing" with the president, Taft went into "a towering rage" and immediately ordered that the gossip stop. In fact, anyone who was caught sharing stories of the "Thing" would be fired.[170]

During Taft's term as president, the household "was shaken by a ghost scare from cellar to rafters."[171] Perhaps because of Taft's concern about White House ghost stories making their way to the American public and because Taft was the first United States president buried in Arlington National Cemetery, there are not many ghostly tales to share. After all, he had a reputation to uphold. His legacy continues through his grave marker, which is surrounded by trees and shrubs in section 30. The memorial is quite stunning. The fourteen-foot-tall monument with classical Greek designs and gold-leafed inscriptions is made from dark mahogany granite from Stony Creek, Connecticut. There are two granite benches on each side of the monument. A walkway to the grave was later added by the cemetery. The memorial was designed and completed in 1932 by American sculptor James

The grave of President William Howard Taft, Arlington National Cemetery. *Author's collection.*

Earle Fraser. Taft's widow, Helen Herron Taft, commissioned the piece, and it was paid for by the Taft family.[172]

When Taft, who is remembered frequently for his weight—or perhaps haunted by it—became chief justice, he had lost considerable weight and had created a fitness regimen of walking three miles from his home to the Capitol each day. On his walk home, he took Connecticut Avenue and crossed over Rock Creek. The bridge was renamed the Taft Bridge in his honor after his passing. Perhaps Taft's ghost is simply walking over the bridge, too focused on his daily routine to compete with stories of the "Thing."

PRESIDENTS AND THEIR GHOSTLY GUESTS: JOHN F. KENNEDY

John F. Kennedy, the thirty-fifth president of the United States, was assassinated in Dallas, Texas, on November 22, 1963. Vice President Lyndon B. Johnson assumed the office of the presidency immediately. He glorified his predecessor, stating that Kennedy would "live on in the immortal words and works he left behind."[173] With Kennedy's figurative ghost hanging over the next president's term and lingering in the hearts and minds of American citizens, why wouldn't his ghost be found in Arlington National Cemetery? Short answer: Kennedy's ghost is too busy haunting a Massachusetts seafood restaurant—more specifically, the Union Oyster House. The restaurant was established in 1826, and it's where the toothpick was first used in the United States. Its website shares the long history of the establishment and its connection to the former president, who patronized the restaurant for years. Kennedy even has a plaque on his favorite booth that dubs it "The Kennedy Booth."[174] There are stories of President Kennedy's ghost appearing in the dining room and even in the restroom, where patrons have looked into the mirror to see the president's image reflected.[175]

Although you aren't likely to see a presidential ghost at Arlington National Cemetery, you should still visit President Kennedy's grave.

> *The initial plot was 20 feet by 30 feet and was surrounded by a white picket fence. During the first year after Kennedy's death, up to 3,000 people per hour visited his gravesite, and on weekends an estimated 50,000 people visited. Three years after Kennedy's death, more than 16 million people had visited the gravesite.*
>
> *Because of the large crowds, cemetery officials and members of the Kennedy family decided that a more suitable site should be constructed. Construction began in 1965 and was completed on July 20, 1967. An eternal flame, lit by Mrs. Kennedy, burns from the center of a five-foot circular granite stone at the head of the grave.*
>
> *The Kennedy family paid actual costs in the immediate grave area, while the federal government funded improvements in the surrounding area that accommodated the visiting public. The 1965 Public Works appropriation included $1,770,000 for this purpose.*[176]

The grave of President John F. Kennedy with Arlington House in the background. *Author's collection.*

EERIE EXTRA: ARLINGTON HOUSE

While visiting the grave of President Kennedy, visitors can get a good, safe view of Arlington House. It's safe because it keeps you distanced from the many restless ghosts of the past that still call this place home.[177] Of course, you're welcome to enter the house if you're not afraid of the spooky apparitions. National Park Service personnel will guide you through the difficult history of the land before it was turned into a cemetery.

19

Ball's Bluff Battlefield and National Cemetery

Route 7
Leesburg, VA 20176

Keeping with the theme of military burial, forty miles northwest of Arlington National Cemetery is Ball's Bluff Battlefield Regional Park, affiliated with NOVA parks, and the Ball's Bluff National Cemetery, which is located at the approximate center of the Union line in that battle. This park was the location of one of the largest Civil War engagements in Loudoun County. Today, visitors can take guided tours, witness living history or simply take a hike along one of the numerous trails with historic signage.

The park entrance is located at the end of what looks like a turnaround with a gravel road that takes visitors to a parking lot with historic signage and maps of the various trails. On June 12, 2024, I visited the park with the intention of heading directly to the national cemetery. Although I was alone, there were numerous hikers, including families and those with dogs. It was a hot day, and most visitors stuck to the wooded trails. I walked on the road in the open field toward the national cemetery. Battlefields have always felt a bit eerie to me, and while walking, I thought about the supernatural accounts of the location, including phantom footsteps and shadowy figures. I even scared myself when I gazed off into the woods and thought I saw someone kneeling on one of the paths. I kept watching and walking, and the figure did not move a muscle. What I thought could be a kneeling apparition turned out to be an old tree stump! It certainly had my heart racing.

Other haunting reports include unexplained screams and a violently shaking tree that was allegedly the site of a Confederate soldier's grave. As

Ball's Bluff Battlefield and National Cemetery, Leesburg. *Author's collection.*

the story is told, he was buried among strangers due to his faith prohibiting him from being buried in his home cemetery.

I did not hear anything but birds and a few barking dogs. The cemetery was small and tidy, surrounded by a stone wall. While the battlefield spooked me, the cemetery did not. The iron gate's historic plaque reads, "Established 1865, Interments 54, Known 1, and Unknown 53." To the right is a tablet engraved with the "Gettysburg Address." In the cemetery are the remains of soldiers who died during the Battle of Ball's Bluff interred in twenty-five graves, with the only known soldier being James Allen of Company H, Fifteenth Massachusetts Infantry. The military markers are set in a curved-inward formation, almost the shape of a horseshoe, with each military marker holding a small American flag.

20
SHARON CEMETERY

EAST FEDERAL STREET
MIDDLEBURG, VA 20117

From the national cemetery, travel approximately twenty miles southwest to reach Middleburg's Sharon Cemetery. Established in 1849, the cemetery is located next to Middleburg Baptist Church, which, after the Second Battle of Manassas, served as a hospital for Confederate soldiers. Many of those who died in the makeshift hospital are buried next door. The cemetery shares land with and borders Emmanuel Cemetery, Baptist Church and Cemetery and Memorial Cemetery. I did not find any distinguishable markers noting where one cemetery began or ended.

A memorial to the Confederate soldiers was erected by the United Daughters of the Confederacy in the center of a circle that has eighty markers surrounding it. Some of the markers contain details, like "Lt. John Tiffany, Co. D. 27th. Va. Regt. Stonewall Brigade, Died July 23, 1863, Aged 21 years & 11 days," while others only include the deceased's initials and last name. While walking through the cemetery, I found the grave of Charles Minnigerode, a familiar name who was the son of Captain Charles Ernest Minnigerode, the elder son of the Reverend Charles Minnigerode, the rector of St. Paul's Church in Richmond who was the College of William & Mary professor who introduced the German custom of the Christmas tree to Williamsburg. History was around every corner of Sharon Cemetery.

An article in *Middleburg Life* shares some of the spookier tales, including one about the lady in white, an apparition that has been seen near a local funeral home.[178] While that is certainly eerie, I was more interested in the tale of a young man who chose not to go to war who continues to haunt the cemetery. The individual was J.T. Morrison, a young man from a wealthy

Sharon Cemetery, Middleburg. *Author's collection.*

family who, instead of going to war like the other men his age, avoided the gunfire and studied law. Although Morrison did not serve as a soldier, it was hard not to be affected by the war that touched neighbors and friends. Perhaps from guilt, feeling like he didn't serve his region, Morrison was consumed by a depression, and it is said that he never left town. The ghost of Morrison has been seen in the cemetery long after the war. Although the article did not explicitly note that Morrison was buried in Sharon Cemetery, I searched for him. I did not find his grave; instead, I noticed one of the graves in the Confederate circle reads J.W. Morrison—likely coincidence but still a poignant one.

THE OMINOUS END

With more tales of Civil War soldiers seemingly not yet at rest, unidentified screams and whistling, strange creatures and even a ghostly slap, the ghosts of Northern Virginia might just keep you up at night. Again, these are only a few of the haunting stories; there is much more to uncover here, but the ghosts beckon us to continue our journey. Our next tour stop is Tidewater and Coastal Virginia, where we'll encounter the commonwealth's oldest known burials.

PART III

TIDEWATER AND COASTAL VIRGINIA

Flowing through this region are major rivers that rise and fall with the tide from the ocean. There is no question about where the region got its name. Tidewater is the eastern region of Virginia and includes the Chesapeake Bay and the Eastern Shore. If we headed farther east, we would be in the Atlantic Ocean. Today's visitors will find colonial and Civil War–era memorials and museums, along with Virginia Beach and Great Dismal Swamp. Tidewater also includes Virginia's oldest known gravesites from English settlers, and it includes quite a spectacle of specters.

21

Westover Plantation Cemetery

Charles City, VA 23030

Westover Plantation is a 1,025-acre historic plantation located on the James River. William Byrd II, the founder of Richmond, is believed to have built the mansion around 1730. The house is noted for its symmetry. The secret passages make Westover a great backdrop for a ghostly tale, and it has a few. But for our tour, we're going to focus on the grounds.

Byrd died at Westover in 1744 and was buried in the garden. Not far from his memorial is the location of the original Westover Parish Church and Cemetery, established in 1625. The cemetery is a quarter mile from the house. It is here that his eldest daughter, Evelyn Byrd (1707–1737), was buried. It's a tranquil setting surrounded by trees, and it's near the poplar grove where she used to walk. Yet Evelyn does not seem to rest. Some believe that a broken heart during her short life might have led her to linger in this world with some unfinished business, although the accounts of her ghost being sighted suggest she is a friendly, peaceful spirit.[179] Might Evelyn be holding on to something other than love?

As the story is told, Evelyn and her dear friend Anne Carter Harrison of Berkeley seemed enchanted by the idea of connecting to those in the afterlife and made a promise to each other that the first one to die would try to return to visit the other "in such a fashion not to frighten anyone."[180] When Evelyn passed away first, Anne believed that her friend had indeed kept her promise. Anne first saw her friend walking the property near the cemetery as if she had never left.

Evelyn Byrd's box tomb can be seen at the front. Westover Plantation Cemetery, Charles City. *Author's collection.*

Since that first sighting, the ghost of Evelyn Byrd has been seen by several visitors. What is curious about the ghost is that it does not appear as a transparent apparition but rather as a living person. Witnesses mistake the ghost for a visitor who seemingly disappears, leaving them more puzzled than frightened.[181]

Ghost stories can be derived from the state of a cemetery or even the peculiarity of a grave marker. The cemetery is well kept, but there is something about Evelyn Byrd's tombstone that might appear a bit ominous to an unfamiliar eye. Her memorial is a chest tomb, or box tomb, that looks like a rectangular jewelry box, albeit much larger. In the United States, bodies are not frequently found within the box portion; instead, they were buried underneath.

Her epitaph reads:

> *Here in the Sleep of Peace Reposes the Body of Mrs. Evelyn Byrd Daughter of the Hon. William Byrd Esq. The various & excellent Endowments of Nature Improved and perfected by an accomplished Education Formed her For the Happyness of her Friends: For an Ornament of her Country; Alas*

> *Reader! One can detain nothing however valued From unrelenting Death: Beauty, Fortune, or exalted Honour! See here a Proof! And be reminded by this awfull Tomb that every worldly Comfort flees away Excepting only what arises from imitating the virtues of our Friends and the contemplation of the Happyness To which God was pleased to call this Lady on the 13th Day of November 1737, In the 29th year of her Age*

Evelyn's box tomb appears to be held together by a metal brace that secures the stone pieces and keeps the sides from collapsing. This is an early example of historic preservation saving the memorial, although it could easily be misunderstood as an attempt to hold something inside the tomb. What might be seen as a haunting image in a Gothic tale is more a lesson in appreciation—nothing tangible, not even an exquisite memorial, lasts forever. Yet the ethereal reminder of the promise between two young friends who vowed to return from the grave continues to haunt visitors of Westover.

22
WESTOVER PARISH CEMETERY

6401 JOHN TYLER MEMORIAL HIGHWAY CHARLES CITY, VA 23030

Approximately one and a half miles north of Historic Westover is the Westover Episcopal Church Cemetery that was built at its current location around 1730. Today, the church is a welcoming community; its history has included lapses in church services due to the politics of the time.

> *The end of support by public taxation at the start of the Revolutionary War, along with the disestablishment of the Church in 1784 and widespread prejudice against Anglicans as English loyalists, were devastating to all Anglican Churches at the time. Bereft of clergy who had fled for their safety, congregations and parish lands were confiscated or abandoned.*[182]

Westover Parish's long history includes abandonment, which makes it the perfect setting for a ghost story. Its history is also connected to United States presidents who worshipped here, including George Washington, Thomas Jefferson, William Henry Harrison, John Tyler and Theodore Roosevelt. The history can still be sensed as one walks through the churchyard. Yet my visit to the churchyard was focused on visiting the grave of Ms. Elizabeth "Lizzie" Rowland, the late daughter of Spencer Rowland, who built Edgewood, which she allegedly haunts.

DuPont Lee wrote, "Large and substantially built, Edgewood's atmosphere is that of comfort and cheer. Tall chimneys suggest hospitable fires when the winds of winter blow, and the great oaks speak of grateful share in

Edgewood Plantation, Charles City. *Author's collection.*

summertime."[183] During March 17 and March 18, 2023, just under two miles from Westover Parish Cemetery, I booked Lizzie's room in Edgewood, "an opulent bed & breakfast inn that features stunning interiors, rich upholstery, lavish canopy beds, gold-gilded frames, lace and damask window treatments, and a double free-standing winding staircase."[184] Edgewood is now owned by Dot and Julian Boulware, who purchased the historic property in 1978.[185] Pirok wrote, "Virginia homebuyers knew that the old homes were valuable and unique because they held stories that defined the homes as places and transformed homeowners into local historians and elites by association."[186] This is true for both Dot and Julian, who recounted the stories that they had heard about the hauntings, as well as their own experiences.

At the time, I was teaching a course on ghost stories and haunted history and thought a short stay in a haunted room with a view was just what I needed. The home is old, and the floors are crcaky, something that I will always prefer to pay for over a sterile room in a hotel chain. I want charm and history. Of course, at the time, I did not realize that Lizzie had died in the room where I was planning to sleep.

As the legend is told, Lizzie Rowland waited so long in that room that she etched her name in the glass of the upstairs bedroom window

Left: The grave of Elizabeth "Lizzie" Rowland, Westover Parish Cemetery, Charles City. *Author's collection.*

Below: The signature of Elizabeth "Lizzie" Rowland in the window in Edgewood, Charles City. *Author's collection.*

while watching and listening for the sounds of her lover's "spirited horse" returning him to her.[187] She died of a broken heart after he did not return from the war. Legend has it that she still waits for him and watches from her upstairs window. Some witnesses note her "frail" form, while others share that she "is dressed in white and holds a candle."[188] The property owners shared their haunted stories, including Lizzie sightings and how pictures will randomly fall from the walls. They also shared stories about the hundreds of visitors who have come to witness Lizzie, although DuPont Lee's witness stated, "The ghost never roams when anyone is at home, but only when she has the place to herself. Possibly her Spirit is awakened by the hoofbeats on the road of some passing traveller [*sic*]."[189] Looking out the window, I saw vehicles pass by, but sadly, I saw no horses. That did not feel promising for a personal experience.

Staying in Lizzie's room was a bit eerie. In the middle of the night, I awoke feeling as if someone was watching me. I did not want to open my eyes. When I finally did, there was only darkness.

Before checking out, I made sure that I stood by Lizzie's window for several minutes in the hopes that someone in a passing car would get a glimpse of me and mistake me for the ghost.

23
Pet Cemetery at Sherwood Forest

14501 John Tyler Memorial Highway
Charles City, VA 23030

This next stop on our tour takes us to Sherwood Forest, the home of the tenth president of the United States, John Tyler. The property comprises 1,600 acres, and the buildings were established starting in 1680 through 1850. President Tyler retired here with his wife, Julia Gardiner Tyler, in 1845. When I learned that there was a pet cemetery and another gray lady connected to the land associated with a president, I could not wait to visit. It turns out that there were more than just some ghost stories about a gray lady; Sherwood Forest has "strong psychic phenomena," including a premonition of death that came true.[190]

I first set out to visit the pet cemetery at Sherwood Forest on March 18, 2023. It's one of the most amazing pet cemeteries I've ever seen due to its statuary and the humor behind some of its epitaphs. The memorials are dedicated to cats; dogs, including the president's dog Le Beau; goats; and horses, including Mrs. Tyler's horse Beau Meahr and President Tyler's favorite pet, his horse named General.

General's epitaph reads:

> *Here lie the bones of my old horse, "General,"*
> *Who served his master faithfully*
> *For twenty-one years,*
> *And never made a blunder.*
> *Would that his master could say the same!*

Pet cemetery at Sherwood Forest, Charles City. *Author's collection.*

Along with memorials noting specific pets, the cemetery is filled with statues of dogs, cats, horse heads, birds, praying angels, a duck and goats. I encourage visitors to take their time to read the epitaphs. My favorites were two markers for family goats. One epitaph reads, "Percival was NOT a pygmy goat," which must have been an inside joke, while another reads, "William the Cantankerous Butthead." I can just imagine William's personality.

PRESIDENTS AND THEIR GHOSTLY GUESTS: JOHN TYLER

The brochure points out President Tyler's "chosen gravesite." It reads, "The President died in Richmond at the first meeting of the Confederate Congress, of which he was a member. Due to the Union invasion of Charles City County, he was, of necessity, buried in Richmond at Hollywood Cemetery. A magnificent 15' marble marker, erected by the people of the United States of America, marks his gravesite."

The chosen location of Tyler's grave is next to the pet cemetery. The area was marked off with a partition to respect the sanctity of what was

President John Tyler's "Chosen Gravesite" at Sherwood Forest, Charles City. *Author's collection.*

supposed to be Tyler's final resting place. Trees dot the land, and from that location, there is a nice view of the house where Tyler lived with his wife and seven children.

It might be at this chosen gravesite that visitors can get a glimpse of the gray lady, the apparition who freely moves about the house and the grounds. The gray lady has been seen moving about in various parts of the house and gardens and has been heard rocking in a rocking chair that is not visible.

Although the apparition of the gray lady is highlighted in magazines in the fall, Mrs. Tyler's premonition highlights the psychic energy that reverberates through the land. As the story is told, in January 1862, Tyler went to Richmond to attend a conference. His wife and their new baby were to join him the following week. Mrs. Tyler had a terrible nightmare where she saw her husband dying in a large bed with an eagle carved into the headboard. The dream was vivid and alarming. She immediately traveled to Richmond, where she found Tyler perfectly healthy and perhaps somewhat amused over her concerns from a dream. However, within days, Tyler suffered a sudden illness and died in a bed at the Exchange Hotel—a bed that perfectly matched the one in Mrs. Tyler's dream.[191]

Traveling twenty miles east to Williamsburg, it may feel like we're traveling back in time as we tour one of the oldest colleges in the United States.

24

College Cemetery of William and Mary

James Blair Drive
Williamsburg, VA 23186

The College of William & Mary was founded in 1693 by the royal charter of King William III and Queen Mary II of England. It is the second-oldest institution of higher learning in the United States, and the Sir Christopher Wren Building, one of the university's main halls, is the oldest college building still in use in America. The building and the grounds are also said to be haunted, and considering its history with war and use as a hospital for sick and injured soldiers, three fires that devastated the structure requiring it to be rebuilt and the crypt under the chapel that has been disturbed several times, residual hauntings seem inevitable. Fortunately, the university does not shy away from sharing its ghost stories.

> *Ghost stories are common at universities across the globe, but when you have a colonial history spanning three centuries and a campus tinged with stories of piracy and war, you're bound to have more than a few creepy stories.*[192]

The campus is just blocks from historic Williamsburg, the historic jail and the first American hospital focused on treating the mentally ill, the Public Hospital of Williamsburg. The area has a history of witch accusations and trials, slavery and the desecration of churches and burial grounds, including that of First Baptist Church, a historic Black church that was located on Nassau Street, and the Native burial ground that was destroyed by the construction of the Colonial Parkway Tunnel.[193]

The Wren building at the College of William & Mary, Williamsburg. *Author's collection.*

The campus has been touched by war. The school was closed in May 1861 through the fall of 1865 due to the Civil War. The Battle of Williamsburg occurred on May 5, 1862, and Union troops occupied the city and the campus for the remainder of the war. The Wren Building, as well as other locations on and off campus, were used as hospitals. Mass graves were used to bury those soldiers who died from war and disease. There were even amputation pits, where discarded limbs were buried.[194]

The Wren Building is considered the most haunted building on campus and houses several ghosts. Reports include apparitions of soldiers, possibly those who died in the building, and disembodied footsteps being heard throughout the halls.

The crypt was included in the south wing when it was added between 1728 and 1732. While the area is called "the crypt," it is a burial place below the floor of the chapel, where it is believed twelve individuals connected to the college were laid to rest. The space is not large enough for anyone to walk around in, and the area is not accessible to the public. Unfortunately, these graves have been disturbed, and in some cases, the bodies were desecrated.

College Cemetery of William & Mary, Williamsburg. *Author's collection.*

When the Wren Building burned in 1859, the burials were exposed. After the fires, there were reports of grave robbery. Diary entries from a Union soldier mention that he "happen[ed] upon the exposed graves and remov[ed] some of the hardware from Lord Botetourt's coffin." These pieces were returned to the college in the twentieth century.[195] Rumors of break-ins from curiosity seekers note that they access the crypt by crawling through the steam tunnels. More disturbing is that bones and other artifacts from the crypt have been taken and not returned, and many have left their marks on the crypt in the form of graffiti.[196]

Just a short walk from the Wren Building, College Cemetery is located behind Tucker Hall, which is also haunted by the ghost of a former student who continues to be stressed about exams. The cemetery was established on January 18, 1859, for the burials of faculty and students. President Benjamin S. Ewell was granted permission to reinter his family members in College Cemetery, and the Ewell monument was erected.[197] The cemetery is enclosed by a brick wall and includes fewer than a half-dozen markers. The largest is the obelisk for Lucian Minor, a law professor who passed in 1858. The marker of President Benjamin Stoddert Ewell, who passed in 1894, is a modest headstone in the back of the cemetery. Being so close to other haunted campus sites, one may not be able to differentiate the locations the apparitions haunt. Reports of ghostly sightings near the cemetery may simply be hauntings from the campus grounds.

25

Bruton Parish Church

201 West Duke of Gloucester Street
Williamsburg, VA 23185

Just a short walk from the College of William & Mary is Bruton Parish Church Cemetery, which has been a burial ground since the seventeenth century. Wooden crosses once marked the graves, as only the wealthiest citizens could afford to ship gravestones from England. Prominent individuals from the area were buried here, including the children of Martha Dandridge Custis, who married George Washington. Letitia Smith, the daughter of the tenth U.S. president, John Tyler, is also buried here.[198] A glance at the tomb of Governor Edward Nott (1657–1706), with a carved skull and a lowered curtain, signifying the curtain of life being lowered, adds to the atmosphere. This churchyard has numerous legends and stories, some of which are strange and others that are quite spooky.

Lightning Never Strikes Thrice?

The first story involves the grave of legal scholar and author Nathaniel Beverly Tucker (1784–1851) who was buried west of the walled entrance of the churchyard. This ghostly tale has more to do with pareidolia, a phenomenon that causes us to perceive faces or shapes when looking at random images. For example, if I looked at a cloud, I might see a bear. Our brains are inclined to recognize patterns and search for meaning. To understand the story to its fullest, I need to share some backstory.

Above: The grave of Governor Edward Nott in Bruton Parish Cemetery, Williamsburg. *Author's collection.*

Left: The obelisk for Nathaniel Beverly Tucker, Bruton Parish Churchyard, Williamsburg. *Author's collection.*

In 1809, Tucker began practicing law, but it wasn't until the 1830s that he began writing poetry, essays and book reviews for the *Southern Literary Messenger.*[199] While working as a law professor, Tucker wrote *George Balcombe* (1836), which was called "the best American novel" by Edgar Allan Poe.[200] The two writers admired each other's talents, and there is even a legend that Tucker wanted a black raven placed on his grave as a tribute to Poe.

Tucker died on August 26, 1851, at the age of sixty-six. His memorial is an obelisk that is located in the bricked sidewalk portion of the churchyard. Even if the premises are closed for the day, Tucker's marker can be easily seen by looking over the churchyard wall. A visitor might prefer to gaze upon the stone during the day, although they should perhaps not get too close, because the legend says that the marker has been struck multiple times by lightning. These lightning strikes did not damage the marker but caused some discoloration that has remained on the stone. Witnesses have reportedly seen the shadowy image of a face in the discoloration. Depending on who you ask, the face belongs to one of two famous individuals—either Abraham Lincoln or Edgar Allan Poe.[201]

While the connection to Poe makes sense, I wonder if there was some historical misunderstanding with Tucker and his nephew Nathaniel Beverley Tucker (1820–1890), who was named after him. His nephew Tucker was on the Union's "Wanted List," and he was even accused of being a conspirator in the assassination of Lincoln.[202] Perhaps knowing this might help you determine the identity of the ghostly face for yourself. Personally, I could make out the face of Lincoln, but I also saw a dog that looked like a smiling pit bull terrier.

STOP DIGGING IN THE CHURCHYARD!

Depending on the context, digging in a churchyard might not seem unusual; it is odd when the digging is focused on finding hidden treasure instead of misplaced bodies. The first story that I found of digs occurring in Bruton Churchyard, both authorized and unauthorized, comes from *The Daily Press* in 1938, which begins, "Digging was resumed this week in Bruton Parish Churchyard in an attempt to find manuscripts to prove that Sir Francis Bacon was ghost writer for Shakespeare."[203] It was believed that "valuable manuscripts were brought to Jamestown before 1630 and later buried in Bruton churchyard." Nothing appears to have been found, but this did not deter believers who played the long game, waiting for their next chance to grab a shovel.

Authorized digs occurred again in 1998, when the churchyard was closed in connection with the Colonial Williamsburg Foundation. This was done only after two unauthorized attempts were made in 1992. Both digs were conducted to look for a secret vault buried in the churchyard that allegedly contains "Sir Francis Bacon's recipe for a new era of spiritual enlightenment" that had "to be found before the millennium."[204]

DISEMBODIED FOOTSTEPS

Next to the churchyard is the George Wythe House, built in the 1750s. This was the home of George Wythe, a signer of the Declaration of Independence, and it is believed to be the most haunted place in Williamsburg. Having a graveyard next door does not help its reputation. Many of the stories of the Wythe House become intertwined with the Bruton Churchyard. Sounds of voices and footsteps are heard, while "shadowy figures walk the house's darkened hallways."[205] This location's stories are vastly varied.

One story that I have heard numerous times on Williamsburg ghost tours is the tragedy of Lady Ann Skipwith. She was married to Sir Peyton Skipwith, a wealthy planter. The two were attending a ball at the Governor's Palace, and for an unknown reason, Lady Skipwith left the ball abruptly. Imagine the scene as a lady in evening attire hurried out into the street unaccompanied. To make matters worse, the strap on her shoe, or perhaps one of her heels, broke. As she ran toward the George Wythe House, again next to Bruton Parish Churchyard, Lady Skipwith entered the house. A loud clacking sound from the broken shoe, which is allegedly still heard today, resounded as she ascended the staircase, where the couple must have been staying. The storyteller always hints at the possibility of Lady Skipwith being angered by learning of an illicit relationship between her husband and sister.

DuPont Lee told the tale a bit more eloquently:

> *From the musty pages of an old prayer book, still treasured by the Randolphs, may be learned that in 1791, at Corotoman, her daughter, Lelia Skipwith, born in 1767, married St. George Tucker. It comes to us that her husband was Sir Peyton Skipwith....He married Ann, daughter of Hugh Miller, and secondly her sister Jean. The record of his faithfulness does not reach us entirely without blemish. The marriage service shortly after the burial beneath the shadow of Bruton Church occasions ground for belief that jealousy was the cause of Lady Skipwith's suicide.*[206]

In DuPont Lee's version, readers learn that Lady Skipwith's dress is a cream satin, and her shoes were "tiny red slippers, upon which shone buckles of brilliants."[207] The haunting sounds that resonate are not from any broken clasp but simply "the music of the little red slippers upon the stairway," as well as the "swish of her silken petticoats…[heard] in the twilight."[208] Sights and sounds of the ghost of Lady Skipwith in the Wythe House, where she ended her life, and in Bruton Cemetery, where she was buried, were embellishments added by later storytellers.

In the version told by L.B. Taylor Jr., he emphasizes that researchers at Colonial Williamsburg say that DuPont Lee's story is not accurate.[209] Lady Skipwith did not die by suicide; rather, she died in childbirth. She was not even buried in Bruton Churchyard. Taylor adds that the story could hint at jealousy, since Sir Peyton did, in fact, marry Lady Ann's sister Jean.[210]

Jackie Eileen Behrend offers a different explanation for the ghostly sightings and sounds of the footsteps. She wrote that after the siege of Yorktown, George Washington used the Wythe House as his headquarters, and after the siege, dozens of wounded men who had fallen in battle used the house as a temporary hospital, including a young French soldier named Colonel Oscar LaBlanc. While he was recovering, he suddenly took a turn for the worse. Fortunately for him, a local woman named Katherine Anderson took notice and watched over him night and day. She had dreams of his recovery and their marriage. Sadly, Oscar died, and Katherine's heart was broken. She, too, passed. "For decades, workers and tourists alike have become frighteningly aware of a ghostly presence that lurks [in the house]. Many have heard voices and footsteps coming from the second floor. At night, shadowy figures walk the house's darkened hallways."[211]

I've often wondered if some of the Williamsburg ghost stories become interwoven because there simply are so many. The next story also includes sightings of a first wife's ghost in Bruton Churchyard.

ROMANCING THE GRAVESTONE

The final story I'll share from Bruton Churchyard is another that must have been enhanced throughout the years. The story is about the tombstones of Reverend Scervant Jones and his wife—or rather, wives. The story "Romance Revealed by Graves in Old Bruton Churchyard" in the 1938 edition of *The Virginia Gazette* reads more like a love story with a bad ending. What the newspaper article and the contemporary online stories share is that Reverend Jones (1785–1854) and his first wife, Ann Timson Buckner Jones (1787–1849), were buried in Bruton Churchyard.

The older version of the tale gives a much richer picture of Reverend Jones, who was "described as a man of singular mixture of piety, simplicity, humor, and business shrewdness."[212] He was a Baptist minister who "held Sunday services in the Powder Horn, known as the Magazine, the building which now faces the old market square on Duke of Gloucester Street" that was near the Methodist church on Francis Street. The article shares some of Reverend Jones's humor. One example comes from him giving grace before a meal:

Good Lord of Love look from above
And bless this 'owl
Which ate this fowl,
And left the bones
For Scervant Jones.

Reverend Jones was said to be a traveler, so it does not seem unusual that when his wife passed, he headed to Richmond to purchase a tombstone for her. Since the trip to and from Richmond was arduous, Reverend Jones decided to set up a temporary home while the marble cutter completed their work.

The epitaph he had planned for Ann's grave was quite poetic and called her his "Angel Wife":

Here lie all that the grave can claim of
Mrs Ann Timson Jones
Consort of the Rev Scervant Jones
Born 1 Sep 1787
Married 26 Dec 1805
Baptized 3 Mar 1822
Died 6 June 1849
If woman ever yet did well
If woman ever did excell
If woman Husband ere adored
If woman ever loved the Lord:
If ever Faith and Hope and Love
In Human flesh did live and move
If all the graces ere did meet
In her, in her they were complete.

My Ann, my all, My Angel Wife
My dearest one, my love, my life.
I cannot say or sigh Farewell.
But where thou dwellest I will dwell.

It was at this time, while he waited in Richmond, that Reverend Jones met and began courting a widow, Mrs. Pollard, a young, attractive and wealthy woman. Reverend Jones arranged for a swift marriage to this woman and brought her home to Williamsburg with him after his first wife's tombstone had been carved.

When Reverend Jones passed, he was buried beside his first wife in Bruton Churchyard. While not much detail is known about her, the second Mrs. Jones apparently added her own sense of style to the end of Reverend Jones's epitaph:

Time was when his cheek with life's crimson was flushed
When cheerful his voice was health sat on his brow.
That cheek is now palsied, that voice is now hushed
He sleeps with the dust of his first partner now.

The article concludes by noting that there are no details about when the second wife passed and where she was buried. Researching the October 1850 census for James City, I found Servant Jones listed as a sixty-five-year-old farmer, along with a Fannie Jones, age thirty-eight, and four Pollard children aged ten and under.[213] Fannie may have been the second Mrs. Jones, but the census record is not clear.

This is where the contemporary stories differ. Williamsburg Ghost Tour shares:

Reverend Jones and his wife were expecting their first child. Sadly, there were complications during labor and the doctor informed him that she was not going to survive. While she was on her deathbed, he proclaimed his undying love for her. He told her how he could never imagine life without her, nor could he ever be with another woman, and asked her to wait for him so they could reunite in heaven.[214]

Ghost stories frequently include high-stakes situations, such as childbirth and lost loves; however, Ann Jones died at the age of sixty-one. She would have been much too old to have given birth to a child.

There is a William B. Jones, age twenty-five, listed in the 1850 census. If his mother had been Ann Jones, she would have been thirty-six or thirty-seven at the time of his birth. While that is still considered old for the time, it is much more reasonable than a woman in her sixties giving birth. Williamsburg Ghost Tour continues:

> *Just three months after her death, Reverend Jones rode back into town in a carriage, with his dead wife's tombstone. During this time, witnesses saw the wife, who had died and was buried, roaming the church cemetery grounds, and even sitting in the church pew. It is said that she was patiently waiting to reunite with her husband.*[215]

This version of the story includes a more sinister plot. The ghost of Ann, who had been promised that she would reunite with her husband, haunted the cemetery where she was buried, waiting for her husband to return. Williamsburg Ghost Tour continues:

> *Almost immediately upon the arrival of Reverend Jones and his new wife, people continued to see the apparition of the original Mrs. Jones throughout the church building and the graveyard, only now, she was very upset by the new wife and was seen crying and wailing, angry over his broken oath.*[216]

The ghost is now distraught and seemingly jealous that her husband replaced her. Williamsburg Ghost Tour concludes:

> *To add insult to injury, Rev. Jones had his new wife's grave plot placed in between him and his first wife. Not only did Rev. Jones find a new wife, his resting place is separated from his first wife by another woman. The Joneses are still buried here in Bruton Parish Church's graveyard. Sometimes, late at night, the church organ can be heard playing on its own when nobody is inside. People still hear the anguished cries of Reverend Jones' broken-hearted first wife and see her roaming the graveyard. Additionally, the curtains inside the church flutter and move without explanation.*[217]

It is a heart-wrenching ghost story that simply is not true unless we consider it figuratively. At the time, society must have frowned upon bringing home a second wife and the tombstone of one's first wife in the same trip. I would find it a bit crass now. However, the contemporary story speaks more to society's discomfort with second marriages, especially those that occur after a death. What we can take from this story is that while there are reports of apparitions of weeping women and strange sounds, we frequently look to the grave markers and even the epitaphs to draw conclusions about the origins of these tales. Are we simply uncomfortable witnessing a ghost without knowing the backstory, or is it in our nature to create explanations for ghost sightings? The next ghost story also comes from the Duke of Gloucester Street; it's a cemetery many Colonial Williamsburg visitors may completely overlook.

26

Jones Family Cemetery

East Duke of Gloucester Street
Williamsburg, VA 23185

I first learned of the Jones Cemetery in Colonial Williamsburg in 2016 through the Williamsburg Ghost Tour mobile app. The Jones Cemetery/secretary's office was the last stop on the tour, and it turned out to be my favorite. Today, I always make a point to visit. The family cemetery is located behind a brick wall with a locked iron gate. But this does not stop me from standing on my toes to peep over that wall or from looking through the gate.

There are seven family graveyards in the historic area of Colonial Williamsburg. If you're curious about those other cemeteries, the Colonial Williamsburg Foundation has a "Historic Area Graveyard Study" that goes into more detail.[218]

The graves in front of the secretary's office belong to the members of the Jones family. I have seen the cemetery referenced as Jones Cemetery or as the Secretary's Office Graveyard, although there is no church on the premises. Each grave is composed of a marble slab and an accompanying urn. Each inscription follows a pattern, including the deceased's name, their parents' names and a short verse. The graves do not include birth or death dates. Again, the cemetery is surrounded by a wall and has a locked gate. Many visitors walk right by the brick walls without noticing the small cemetery.

Virginia's first capital was Jamestown, and it was relocated to Williamsburg in 1699. The secretary's office building was established as a safe place to store government documents after a 1747 fire at the capitol building destroyed many public records. This building was made of brick with a stone floor. Without an attic or a basement to collect moisture, the two fireplaces in the

Jones Family Cemetery, Williamsburg. *Author's collection.*

building were intended to keep all of the paper documents dry and mold-free. The building was not needed after the capital was moved to Richmond in 1780.

The secretary's office building later became the residence of David Rowland Jones and Mary Ann Tinsley Jones, along with their children. In the ghost tours that I have taken in Colonial Williamsburg, including the mobile app tour, the secretary's office is most likely a stop because it is part of the Duke of Gloucester Street, and it is right by the old capitol building. There are associated stories as part of the ghost tours and then numerous mentions of paranormal activity. One of the legends says that the Jones family were reclusive and seldom seen anywhere outside of church. They had seven daughters, none of whom were married, as they were not allowed to leave home. The ghost story includes an apparition of a young girl named Edna that is seen running toward the road, as it is told that Edna was killed by a carriage as she tried to secretly go out to meet a suitor. Based on their obituaries, none of the daughters died after being run over by a carriage.

Further, the obituary for Mary Ann Tinsley Jones does not include anything strange about David Rowland Jones or the family, and it does not portray any of them as loners.[219] Quite the contrary, really. For Emma's obituary, it reads that she had "many friends." Helen and Ida were beloved schoolteachers, as was their sister Virginia, who attended the College of William & Mary. Their daughter Mary was involved with civic and religious organizations and was involved in educational work in schools. Of the seven daughters, one was married. Eudora not only married but also gave birth to two daughters and two sons.

Perhaps the ghost story arose from the seemingly unusual location of a family cemetery sitting among numerous tourist attractions, including the former state capitol building. Its placement may surprise many tourists who walk by the brick enclosure without realizing it is a sacred space.

Heading thirty-seven miles southeast along the coast, our tour takes us to another churchyard with a longtime role in American history.

27

St. Luke's Church Cemetery

14477 Benns Church Boulevard
Smithfield, VA 23430

St. Luke's Historic Church Cemetery is Virginia's oldest *open* cemetery that was started as a church graveyard after the church was built in the late seventeenth century. The church is known as the Brick Church, the Old Brick Church and Historic St. Luke's Church, and while local lore dates the church to 1632, historians "suggest a completion date between 1685 and 1687. Architectural historians feel comfortable with the claim that St. Luke's remains Virginia's oldest surviving church building."[220] The oldest marked grave dates to 1767.[221] The church was actively used until 1785, at which time, the Church of Virginia was dissolved. St. Luke's fell into disuse but was restored in 1821.[222]

I visited on August 10, 2024. Visitors enter the church through a wicket door that is a foot off the ground; it was believed this "prevent[ed] evil spirts from entering the church because they only flowed at ground level."[223]

St. Luke's Churchyard is featured in L.B. Taylor Jr.'s *The Ghosts of Virginia.* The story that is passed down says a horseback rider who was caught in a storm decided to use the church in its dilapidated state as a makeshift shelter. He tied up his horse and sat against the wall of the church while he waited for the passing storm when he saw something that he described as "white, fluttering" appearing in the graveyard. The rain obscured his vision, but something appeared to be hovering over an open grave site. This frightened the rider, who quickly disregarded the weather and took off on his horse to find another place to rest. The story is a bit unclear, but it appears that the

St. Luke's Church Cemetery, Smithfield. *Author's collection.*

The grave of Reverend Alexander Norris is located directly below the window, St. Luke's Church Cemetery, Smithfield. *Author's collection.*

frightening white creature was a large goose that had fallen into the grave and could not manage to escape. Frantic fluttering occurred.[224]

One story that is told in the church museum's history video has become a ghost story about Reverend Alexander Norris, who mysteriously "toppled from one of the windows in 1839 breaking his neck and was buried where he laid." Visitors of the churchyard have reported seeing the ghost of Reverend Norris walking near his gravesite. Other ghost stories include a phantom horse-drawn wagon carrying a casket through the churchyard.[225]

By the 1950s, the church had again fallen into disuse and disrepair. Thankfully, the efforts of local residents, including Henry Mason Day, were able to save the church so that it was "declared a national shrine and a Virginia landmark."[226]

For visitors who want a bit more local lore than ghost stories, St. Luke's offers its annual Twilight Cemetery Tours each October. It offers a family-friendly and an adults-only tour that features a hard cider tasting.[227]

Fifteen miles south of Smithfield, our tour takes us to Suffolk, a city that takes the business of storytelling and mysteries quite seriously!

28
CEDAR HILL CEMETERY

NORTH MAIN STREET AND MAHAN STREET
SUFFOLK, VA 23434

Established in 1802 and originally named Green Hill Cemetery, Cedar Hill Cemetery comprises thirty-two acres and has approximately ten thousand burials, including those of prominent individuals from the community as well as veterans from the Civil War, World War I and II, the Korean War and the Vietnam War. It is an official Virginia Civil War Trail site.

The cemetery includes a variety of tombstones and family mausoleums, and today, it offers Suffolk's first scatter garden, allowing families the option of scattering ashes instead of a burial.[228] Cedar Hill Cemetery is known for its beauty. I learned this firsthand when it became part of my room with a view.

Suffolk has a great literary scene. I first attended the Suffolk Mystery Authors Festival in 2018, where I met author Charlaine Harris. I had so much fun that I decided to make a weekend out of the festival in 2019. This was when I first visited Cedar Hill Cemetery. I attended the festival and a Murder Mystery Soirée and took myself on a tour of the cemetery. While I intentionally booked my hotel *near* the cemetery, I had no idea it would be part of my hotel room view. I have never been so glad to be the kind of person who refuses to pay more for a riverfront view! I rose early each morning to stroll the cemetery. The statuary, tombstones and natural elements are all quite stunning. I had not realized on that first visit that Cedar Hill Cemetery is haunted by more than one ghost.

Cedar Hill Cemetery, Suffolk. *Author's collection.*

A lady in white has been seen throughout the cemetery, searching for her lost love. Believed to be the spirit of a woman who died tragically in an accident, the ghost does not realize that she has passed. Another ghostly sighting that has been witnessed both during the day and night is the apparition of a Confederate soldier. The war never ended for this soldier. He walks the cemetery grounds, protecting it from intruders.[229]

If two ghost sightings are not enough for the ghost hunter, the cemetery also includes disembodied sounds. Throughout the cemetery, there are numerous graves of children. The ghost of one of these little ones can be heard crying at night and, at times, during the day.[230]

For visitors who want a bit more history, Suffolk Tourism has a sixteen-page interactive brochure along with a self-guided walking tour that highlights the history of the cemetery.[231] Suffolk Tourism offers the Cedar Hill Cemetery Stroll, a historic walking tour of the cemetery and Legends of Main Street: A Suffolk Ghost Walk, a tour with a costumed guide who shares "tales of unsolved mysteries and unresolved affairs."[232]

Continuing our tour east through Portsmouth, we arrive in Norfolk to visit another churchyard with a longstanding connection to American history.

29

St. Paul's Episcopal Churchyard

201 St. Paul's Boulevard
Norfolk, VA 23510

St. Paul's Episcopal Church was originally the Borough Church. Built in 1739, it is the oldest building in Norfolk and the only one to weather the destruction of the British in 1776. The church building intentionally keeps the cannonball that was fired by Lord Dunmore of the British fleet lodged in its wall with a commemorative plaque. The cannonball apparently fell out of the wall in the 1830s and was later found in the churchyard and returned to its landing place as a reminder of the church's part in American history.[233]

St. Paul's was not just part of the Revolutionary War; it was used by Union troops as their chapel during the Civil War. Famous individuals have visited the church; in 1964, General Douglas MacArthur, the military leader who served in World War I and the chief of staff of the United States Army during the 1930s, had his funeral here before his remains were buried in the MacArthur Memorial.

I visited on August 10, 2024. The churchyard includes a variety of colonial-era tombstones, with the oldest remaining marker belonging to Dorothy Farrell (1649–1673), who died soon after childbirth. Her husband, Major Hubbard Hubert Ferrell, was one of the officers who was wounded in defense of Jamestown during Bacon's Rebellion.

One grave marker for William Harris (1653–1688) has been hung on the side of the brick building in order to preserve it. The marker reads, "Here lyeth ye Body of William Harris who Depted This life ye 8th day of

St. Paul's Episcopal Churchyard, Norfolk. *Author's collection.*

Cannonball fired by Lord Dunmore, January 1, 1776, St. Paul's Episcopal Church, Norfolk. *Author's collection.*

March 1687/8 Aged 35 years," with the date 1687/8 clarifying that the Gregorian calendar had replaced the Julian calendar. Under the inscription is a somewhat primitive image of a skull with crossbones.

The gravestone of William Harris in St. Paul's Churchyard, Norfolk. *Author's collection.*

Walking through such a churchyard connects one to the past. I wonder about the stories that could be told here. One tale that is shared is a ghost story about a haunting figure that has been seen in the graveyard. This ghost has been identified as the spirit of the late Dr. Nicholas Albertson Okeson, who was the rector of St. Paul's for twenty-six years and who may have died in 1882, possibly from malaria.[234] The apparition is said to be seen on the darkest of nights. When history seekers visit the cannonball during the day, perhaps the ghost of Okeson appears to those who find themselves in dark times as a spiritual reminder of the church's past.

Just one mile from St. Paul's Churchyard is another historic cemetery with a somewhat humorous ghostly tale that was shared in a local newspaper.

EERIE EXTRA: ELMWOOD CEMETERY

238 EAST PRINCESS ANNE ROAD
NORFOLK, VA 23510

Elmwood Cemetery was established in 1852 and includes approximately fifty acres with a variety of tombstones and family mausoleums, such as those of the Core and Le Kies families. The Core mausoleum was opened for a special tour on June 30, 2017, and I was fortunate enough to enter to see the artwork.

Much of the funerary iconography in Elmwood comes from the Victorian era. One notable memorial is the bronze angel by American sculptor William Couper that is located near his mother's grave.[235] The angel "record[s] the deceased's name in the book of everlasting life."[236]

Elmwood Cemetery was originally connected to Cedar Grove Cemetery by a bridge across Smith's Creek. This next story comes from a time when a wall was extended around the cemetery and an entrance gate was added, a somewhat significant point about how the cemetery was changing for this next ghost sighting from the *Virginia-Pilot* of December 21, 1902. The story is told by an unnamed merchant and resident of the suburban district who was coming home late one night from the store and was anxious to sit in front of a warm fire, so he decided to take a shortcut through Elmwood Cemetery. In a hurry to avoid any "pocketbook snatchers and footpads issued forth," he kept a good pace through the cemetery, "jumping over mounds and tombstones," when he saw something concerning. Throughout the story, the merchant emphasizes that he was not at all frightened. He explains, "Down in the hollow at one corner of the cemetery, where the trees didn't admit the moonlight, I saw something white rise up out of a grave and then disappear in the earth." Afterward, he heard "a dreadful groan…from a human being undergoing great physical torture." Again, something white rose up from the grave and then disappeared with a groan. Although he was not frightened, the merchant decided that he needed to quickly hurry along

Elmwood Cemetery, Norfolk. *Author's collection.*

and leave the cemetery. When asked if he believed he had seen a ghost, he responded, "I did not believe it was at the time. But I wasn't going to set myself up as a judge and decide the case….I was not going to investigate. It wasn't my business anyhow." Again, the merchant emphasized that he was not scared; he just wanted to find a quiet place to reflect on what he had seen. When asked if he had run from the cemetery, he says, "Well—er, yes, I must have run." To avoid humiliation, he added, "It was a good story, and I was anxious to get home and tell my wife about it."[237]

THE OMINOUS END

With some of Virginia's oldest known gravesites, a haunted college, ghostly tales of love and friendship and history spanning centuries, this region is hard to exit. Like the perfect residual haunting, the energy of this region has been imprinted on my heart. I want to return again and again, but we still have more regions of Virginia to explore. The ghosts are calling us. I can just hear them over the mountains.

Part IV

Blue Ridge and Southwest Virginia

Many visitors to this region, often abbreviated SWVA, come to see the birthplace of country music and travel the Crooked Road, while other visitors come to experience the Blue Ridge Parkway, called "America's most scenic drive." The New River, credited with being the oldest river in North America, flows through this region. This westernmost area of Virginia is rural and closely connected to Appalachian culture. While the creative economy of recreation and tourism have added to its economic development, the coalfields, the area where coal can be mined, have helped with economic expansion in the area. Of course, we're here to learn the ghost stories of the region's cemeteries. We will start in Lynchburg at one of my favorite cemeteries—and it's not a favorite *just* because it has the smoothest gliding tree swing! I highly recommend you take a moment to sit on that swing. You won't regret it.

30
OLD CITY CEMETERY

401 TAYLOR STREET
LYNCHBURG, VA 24501

Established in 1806, Old City Cemetery, which was known as Methodist Cemetery, is located on land donated by John Lynch, the founder of Lynchburg. It is the oldest city-owned cemetery still in use in Virginia and one of the oldest burial grounds in the nation. No one questions that it is haunted. The cemetery includes approximately twenty thousand burials, with three-quarters of those belonging to individuals of African descent, as it was the primary burial site for Black Americans from 1806 to 1865.

While it is an active cemetery, the twenty-seven-acre "gravegarden" also functions as a wedding venue and museum. There is the Victorian Mourning Museum, which displays mourning jewelry, trinkets of remembrance and coffins. There is also the pest house, hearse house, station house and chapel that offer visitors self-guided exhibits with audio recordings and brochures. With a variety of events and museums on the property, the cemetery attracts more than thirty-three thousand visitors annually.[238] Two of my favorite events include its October Candlelight Tours and Scandalous: Lynchburg's 19th-Century Red-Light District. Both of these events highlight the history of the individuals buried in the cemetery.

In 2023, I attended the sixteenth season of the October Candlelight Tours. My tour was the last of the night and the last of the season. It was also right after I packed up my book signing event in the cemetery, so the evening felt extra special. The sky was clear, and the moon was bright in the sky as visitors were led by lantern light. Our spirit guide led us through

Mother and daughter Agnes and Lizzie Langley are buried in this plot surrounded by a wrought-iron fence. The pair ran a "sporting house" in the 1800s. Old City Cemetery, Lynchburg. *Author's collection.*

the cemetery to six vignettes of reenactors of cemetery residents "from beyond the grave" to hear "their fascinating tales of life—and death." The scene actors and spirit guides were phenomenal. The amount of work that went into this event showed in all the details—a great script, skilled actors and performers, as well as parking attendants (Old cemeteries are just not equipped for the size of today's vehicles!), those who placed hundreds of candlelight bags along the paths and the ticket takers. It was one of the best living history events that I've ever witnessed. Actress Makeda Payne brought author Ms. Lizzie Chambers Hall to life. It was quite emotional, especially since she was portraying a woman writer who is not frequently showcased. That is one of the best parts of these candlelight tours—they are not about being spooky or merely spotlighting the who's who of the cemetery. Each year, different cemetery residents are featured after months of research.

I appreciated that the interpretation of history included three examples of Black women who were interpreted through the lens of Black joy. These women's stories included those of Lizzie Chambers Hall, Harriet Burton and Judy Rieves, and they were respected and celebrated. I also thoroughly enjoyed the story of George Liskecomb Wilkinson, who enlisted in the army and earned the rank of sergeant in the U.S. Army Air Corps. Actor Russell Hill played George Wilkinson, which was extra special, since Wilkinson had been the actor's Boy Scout leader when he was young. The tour brought our senses to life with the smell of apple pies that I believe were actually fragrant apple candles (or I missed out on some tasty pie). I even went home with smoke in my hair from the bonfire. It was a magical night that I cannot imagine being topped.

It is when visitors head home and the cemetery staff are having quiet moments to themselves when sensations of nearby apparitions come to life. When I asked one cemetery associate if Old City Cemetery was haunted, a group of volunteers and workers around that associate all responded affirmatively and began citing personal instances in which they knew they were not quite alone, along with times they saw mysterious lights. Although most of the stories of ghosts and disembodied sounds come from those associated with the cemetery, Old City Cemetery is filled with opportunities for volunteers to get involved with gardening, historical research, the cemetery bees, goat feeding and maintenance and other things. Sign up to volunteer, and you might experience your own ghostly encounter.

Our next tour stop is just under two miles away. No need for a behind-the-scenes access pass to the ghosts, the next cemetery includes a resident ghost on its website!

31
SPRING HILL CEMETERY

3000 FORT AVENUE
LYNCHBURG, VA 24501

Spring Hill Cemetery was Lynchburg's first rural cemetery. It was organized in 1852 and designed by John Notman of Philadelphia, who also designed Richmond's Hollywood Cemetery. Its website lists Cornelia Clopton (1852–1917) as its "resident ghost," which made me very curious. Cemetery management do not tend to mention ghosts, and they certainly do not list "ghosts" on their website. Yet here she is listed as one of the notables.[239]

Cornelia L. Clopton was born on October 31, 1852, to Reverend James Chappell Clopton and Mary Ann Cottrell Clopton. She lived nearly all of her days in Lynchburg, and from United States census listings and her death certificate, she remained at home to help take care of her family. Cornelia was one of six children. William Abner Stuart, her oldest sibling, was born on July 25, 1848. Martha Susan was born in 1850, Cornelia was born in 1852, Fannie Fry was born in 1855, John was born in 1860 and Benjamin Ashby was born in 1862, just months before his older brother, William Abner, who was part of Shoemaker's Virginia Horse Artillery, was mortally wounded near Port Royal by Union gunboats. William Abner died on December 6, 1862. He was fourteen years old. Their father, Reverend James Chappell Clopton, died on May 18, 1864. I could not find if his death was connected to the war. Her sister Fannie passed away in 1910 at the age of fifty-five at the Home and Retreat Hospital,[240] and her mother died in 1914. Aside from her mother, who was eighty-nine when she passed, half of the family died relatively young—still not particularly unusual for that time.

The grave of "resident ghost" Cornelia Clopton in Spring Hill Cemetery, Lynchburg. *Author's collection.*

Cornelia passed away from pneumonia on March 26, 1917, in Bozeman, Montana, at the age of sixty-four while visiting her brother. She was buried in Spring Hill Cemetery in Lynchburg, Virginia.[241] Her death certificate lists her cause of death as pneumonia, while some newspaper articles from the 1970s read that she died from the flu. Her two remaining brothers lived in Montana, and her sister Susie Ford lived in Canton, Ohio, at the time of her death.

Cornelia Clopton became part of a ghost story in 1974, when an unnamed man, whom the newspaper gave the fictious name Philip Williams, lived in the family's former residence. Williams and his wife noticed "odd noises" and some "undefinable presence." On the morning of April 5, 1974, he saw a light that he first assumed was the neighbor's garage door until he realized the light source was not coming from that direction. The light took the shape of a five-foot-tall woman with "her hair up and a long skirt and full leg o' mutton sleeves." Williams explained, "The woman never looked up [and] never spoke, but moved slowly to another room, out of sight." After doing some research at the courthouse, they determined it was Cornelia. While historical records are not clear, the belief is that Cornelia Clopton's body arrived from Minnesota on April 5, just fifty-seven years before. Williams also "learned there used to be an early train from the West, arriving in Lynchburg at 5 or 5:20 a.m.," which was the approximate time the apparition was seen. The couple continued to feel her presence about the house but noted, "It was terribly frightening to see…but it's totally benevolent." He concluded, "It's a happy house—always has been."[242]

Cornelia was buried beside her parents, her sister Fannie and her brother William Abner. Even without a map, visitors can easily spot the Clopton graves while strolling through the cemetery, as they are located near the road. But why wasn't Fannie considered the ghost? She died younger than her sister. My best hunch is that when researching the "ghost," Cornelia's Halloween birth date stuck out, along with the fact that she died far from home. Those details made for a better story.

Just under thirteen miles north of Lynchburg is our next tour stop, a haunted college with a haunted cemetery that includes a monument that screams!

SPOOKY SPECIAL

Halloween was celebrated during the Civil War. In October 1861, *Harper's Weekly* published a political cartoon called "Jeff Davis Reaping the Harvest," which depicted a ghoulish image of the Confederate president with a scythe collecting wheat topped with skulls.[243] For young women in Virginia during this time, Halloween was traditionally used as a time to tell the future. In 1896, *The Richmond Dispatch* published a poem titled "Girls on Halloween," which detailed Halloween rituals girls engaged in to conjure up the image of their future husbands.[244]

32

Monument Hill at Sweet Briar

Monument Drive
Sweet Briar, VA 24595

In 1884, Daisy Williams died at sixteen years old. Her mother, Indiana Fletcher Williams, who had inherited a plantation from her parents, passed in 1900, leaving her estate to be transformed into a college for young women in her daughter's honor. Both mother and daughter were buried in Monument Hill, the burial grounds of the Fletcher and Williams families that overlooks the campus of Sweet Briar College.

In 1992, a collection of ghost stories was published by Sweet Briar alumnae. Ann Marshall Whitley wrote, "Most members of the family are buried on the Monument Hill....It is here, perhaps, that one feels the strongest sense of the family's presence," adding, "but some of their spirits have been known to wander and frequent other areas of their former domain."[245] However, it is here in the cemetery that community members hear screams coming from one of the memorials.

In the mid-1990s, a group of four young adults drove up to Monument Hill near midnight. The cemetery must have been very dark, especially after the car's engine and headlights were turned off. The driver was hesitant about being at the cemetery late at night and she was careful to put the car in park and apply the emergency brake. She warned "that she was leaving with or without [the other riders] in five minutes."[246] That did not allow much time for adventure, nor did it allow time for mischief. The group of two women and two men entered the gate to the cemetery. They made their way to Daisy's grave. One young man asked if students did anything special to honor Daisy. One of the women who was a Sweet Briar student cheekily responded that they had to face the monument four times a day and bow to it. At that very moment, one of them noticed that their car had started to roll down the hill. One young man was fast enough to exit the cemetery, catch the runaway vehicle and stop it before anyone was harmed or the car was damaged. After hopping into the moving vehicle, he noticed something odd, especially since the driver had been so serious about taking precautions. Mysteriously, the transmission had been shifted into drive, and the emergency brake was not engaged.[247]

Annually on Founders' Day, at the end of September, students dress in white and pay their respects to the founders by visiting Monument Hill and the Plantation Burial Ground, the cemetery for the enslaved laborers who lived and worked on the grounds. Today, Monument Hill also includes a columbarium with niches available to professors, alumnae and Sweet Briar community members.

I visited on July 25, 2024. I checked in at the gatehouse, received a campus map from security and proceeded to drive to Monument Hill. The campus comprises 2,840 acres, so that Founders' Day Walk is not a short

The monument to Daisy Williams can be seen on the left side of this image. Monument Hill at Sweet Briar. *Author's collection.*

stroll. From Sweet Briar Drive, I turned on Monument Drive, which quickly changes from a paved to a gravel road. I passed a butterfly research garden, a wildflower meadow and a vineyard before I made my way up to the top of Monument Hill. As I approached the circular stone wall that surrounds the cemetery, I parked and walked toward the entrance, where I could see the nearby niches. I was greeted by three deer, including two spotted white-tailed fawns. The view overlooked the campus. This place felt anything but scary until I pushed the old wrought-iron gate open and entered. It was like a secret garden, with blooming crepe myrtles, the sword-like leaves of yucca plants and lush ivy. Yucca plants symbolize mourning, and they are said to be planted in cemeteries to keep restless spirits in their graves.

Inside the stone wall, I felt secluded from campus. I paused and listened for a distinctive whistling or shriek coming from Daisy's "screaming statue" memorial. Allegedly, the hand shape of the monument allows wind to pass through, causing the statue's haunting sound. The wind was blowing, but the sound must have been drowned out by a nearby bees' nest that made the visit ominous in a different way. I could not locate the hive, but the buzzing increased as I carefully walked around the cemetery grounds.

The tallest grave is the monument to Daisy. An angel holding a cross that is wrapped in flowers stands high above the other obelisk and gravestones. The older epitaph reads, "Dedicated in Love to the Sweet Remembrance of Dear Daisy by her Sorrowing Parents James Henry & Indie Fletcher Williams. Requiescat In Pace." There were several coins left behind at her grave, tokens of remembrance. The epitaph at the bottom of the angel statue includes Daisy's name surrounded by stone daisies and the inscription, "Born in Sweet Briar, September 10, 1867 Died Jan 22, 1884."

This is not the original grave marker for Daisy. Daisy's original marker includes a marble angel "[that] guarded [her] grave," and it was moved away from Monument Hill. By 1888, the angel's wing had been broken, presumably by town vandals. The original tombstone was moved to the back of the Sweet Briar Museum.

Many of the ghost stories told at Sweet Briar connect to Daisy and her mother, Indie. The ghosts are seen separately; Daisy's ghost has the reputation of being a prankster who plays tricks on current students, while "Miss Indie's ghost has long been known to hover near the seventh step of the front stairs at Sweet Briar House to protect her former possessions."[248] However, one poignant story told by Martha Stohlman in *The Story of Sweet Briar College* (1956) discusses the house fire of March 1927. From its aftermath, witnesses describe two ghosts coming together:

> *The night was brightened by a full moon. An instructor had gone over to see how the burned house looked by moonlight. As she stood by the sundial in the boxwood circle, she saw a woman and a little girl slowly approach the house, hand in hand, from the garden on the left of the house. They stood for a moment and surveyed the ruin, then…they climbed the steps, passed through the burned doorway, and entered the front hall. The amazed spectator followed quickly to the pace where they had disappeared, but no one was there.…This is the first and only time reported that Daisy and her mother have returned together to the house where they saw so much happiness and grief.*[249]

This reminded the campus community that they were not alone. Their late founder and her daughter, the reason for the establishment of the college, were still there with them in spirit.

Our next tour stop keeps the school spirits alive!

33

Cocke Cemetery at Hollins University

Emerald Lane
Hollins, VA 24019

Hollins University, like so many southern colleges, has its share of ghosts connected to its academic buildings and residential halls. Similar to Sweet Briar, Hollins University also has a cemetery, and the student body has a tradition following convocation in which the seniors visit the graves in Cocke Cemetery to place wreaths there.[250] The school's founder, Charles Lewis Cocke (1820–1901), who led the school for eighty-seven years, is buried here, as is his daughter Martha Louisa "Matty" Cocke (1855–1938), who served as the president of Hollins College and was the first woman president of a Virginia college.[251]

The oldest grave in the cemetery appears to be that of an infant who was born and passed in 1862. The details on the inscription are illegible. The brick wall that surrounds the cemetery was added in 1928. The plaque by the gate reads, "This wall erected in memory of Lucian Howard Cocke by his children." The cemetery is still being used by family members, with a death notice pointing to a private burial in 2020.[252]

I visited Cocke Cemetery at Hollins University on July 21, 2024. The cemetery is not shown on the campus map, although a portion of the access road is shown. When entering the university and turning right on East Campus Drive, there is a steep access road off to the right. I missed it the first time because it comes after a curve. I could see the cemetery's brick wall at a distance and thought I was going to have to hike up the hill. Fortunately, I found the access road, which is a narrow, partially graveled road, and proceeded toward the cemetery. The brick wall surrounds the

Cocke Cemetery at Hollins University. *Author's collection.*

cemetery. A variety of styles of grave markers can be seen, including box tombs, traditional headstones, slant memorials and even a cradle grave.

The cemetery is located up on a hill, a distance away from campus life. Behind the cemetery, one can see only woods. This makes it especially spooky, as there have been reports of lights flickering over the cemetery. Are the spirits of the Cocke family overlooking Hollins University, or could someone or something be visiting the rural cemetery in the darkness? Community members suspect the former, since, after all, this is an academic community. Who would be unwise enough to visit a haunted cemetery in the dark?

EERIE EXTRA: OLD TOMBSTONE CEMETERY

PLANTATION ROAD
HOLLINS, VA 24019

In Tombstone Cemetery in Hollins, the most famous marker is called Old Tombstone, or the Denton Monument, which is in the National Register

The grave of Robert Denton, Old Tombstone Cemetery, Hollins. *Author's collection.*

of Historic Places and the Virginia Landmarks Register. Designed by Laurence Krone, a prolific Virginia-German carver, sometime after 1805, Old Tombstone includes folk art elements that are unique to the area and includes Latin, German and English engravings. It was a monolithic freestone carving, meaning that the memorial was cut from a single piece of material, and it is Krone's only signed work. The memorial was for the young boy Robert Denton, and the grave marker appears in the form of a small coffin with the folk image of a deceased child. Originally, the marker had a removable stone lid that covered the torso and head of the carved child. Due to vandalism, a chain-link fence now surrounds the monument. Unfortunately, this makes the marker challenging to photograph.

I visited Old Tombstone Cemetery on July 21, 2024. I first drove into a parking lot of Northview United Methodist Church before realizing that my GPS was trying to lead me through the woods. The cemetery is located on Plantation Road. There is a small area where you can pull in and park near the entrance gates. The cemetery includes a variety of old gravestones, along with some newer markers. Old Tombstone is located in the back of the cemetery, near the woods. It is completely worth the trip to see a piece of art so original to the area.

34
City Cemetery

501 Tazewell Avenue Southeast
Roanoke, VA 24013

I first read about City Cemetery, also known as City of Roanoke Cemetery, in a social media group, "Roanoke City Cemetery Remembered." The page's pictures from a decade ago show a very different cemetery than the one I visited on July 21, 2024. The pictures show a Victorian cemetery with a variety of memorials, including large cradle graves, obelisks, angel statues and crosses with climbing stone ivy.

The cemetery also appears in L.B. Taylor Jr.'s *Haunted Roanoke* (2013). Taylor writes about a ghost who sits on the wall of a family burial plot, crying. He explains, "The local legend is that she died during the great flu epidemic in 1918. Her husband and children survived her, and when they passed on, they were buried in this plot. The woman's wraith has been witnessed there, crying….She wasn't ready to leave her family so unexpectedly."[253] Another story includes "a mysterious figure lurking in the graveyard late at night. It seems to evaporate when approached."[254]

I first pulled up to the gate, believing that I would be able to drive through the cemetery. The gate was closed and appeared slightly broken. I parked on Tazewell Avenue Southeast. There were a few people walking down the street. As I entered the cemetery, I took a picture of the landscape before I noticed there was a woman sleeping beside a larger marker. I visited in the middle of the day, and it was hot and humid—not a day for a casual nap in the cemetery, if such a thing exists. The woman was dressed in layers and lying directly in the sun. I went to approach her to make sure she was

City Cemetery, Roanoke. *Author's collection.*

alright when I started seeing more people in the cemetery meandering the grounds. I realized that these people were very much alive and unhoused. Some of them, based on their behavior and the paraphernalia near them, were likely taking drugs. There was even someone resting in a cradle grave covered by a tarp.

As a solo traveler in an unfamiliar area, I only felt comfortable visiting the front of the cemetery, near the entrance gates, in case I needed to exit quickly. This was disappointing, because not only was I unable to locate the family plot mentioned in Taylor's book, but I had also hoped to visit the grave of one of Patrick Henry's granddaughters, Maria Antoinette Hambrick.[255]

I researched those who passed and were interred in City Cemetery in 1918 in the hopes that I could include the name of the woman who'd died in a flu epidemic. Of the nine records I found, only three belonged to women. Reviewing their death certificates, none listed influenza as their cause of death. Of the three, only two had children, and only one died before her husband and children. From online photos, that woman may have been buried next to one of her children who passed in 1907, but her other children were buried in other locations. It's unlikely that there would be a wall surrounding their plots, especially since her husband was buried in Richmond.

There are three concerns that I have after visiting City Cemetery. First, the number of unhoused individuals in Roanoke has increased enough to make news headlines, which is a symptom of numerous conditions.[256] The Rescue Mission of Roanoke is next door to the cemetery.[257] They serve breakfast, lunch and dinner and provide shelter and offer an addiction recovery program. However, the mission has limits. It requires money and volunteers. My second concern is about the fate of cemeteries. As families who run cemeteries age and wish to retire, they sometimes have no heirs interested in taking on the business, or when looking for buyers, they are unsuccessful—after that, there are few options left. One of Roanoke's cemetery's board of directors needed to dissolve its nonprofit foundation that has operated its cemeteries for decades and wished to give the properties to the city. Yet the City of Roanoke did not want to take on that responsibility.[258] What will happen to these physical and sacred places? Finally, I am concerned about the "commonwealth's treasury of ghostlore."[259] Reverend W.A.R. Goodwin, who had the idea of restoring Williamsburg, was inspired by the ghost stories and believed that the city needed to be restored because "[the] landscape was no longer a fitting home for the colonial ghosts that remained in the city."[260] Cemeteries are places where stories are told about our past. My research explicitly attempts to give voice to the voiceless spirits and enable others' stories to be told once again. Research allows us to remove some of the silence that occurs with death. Researchers can piece together these stories that came before us, including those from underrepresented groups. Ghostlore is one way that Virginians discuss our difficult past. Without the restoration of the cemeteries as settings for these ghost stories, part of our culture will be lost. Further, it is hard to know if I even saw a ghost in City Cemetery because there were so many living unhoused individuals. I had to focus on the present issues and ignore the past.

Ghost stories, in many ways, are supposed to be fun, but real concerns about the safety and security of the citizens in Roanoke, including those who are unhoused, continue to haunt me. To make a donation to the mission or to volunteer, visit its website, which is listed in the notes.[261]

Head southwest for approximately thirty-five miles, and you'll find the next tour stop—a cemetery with a celebrated dark past.

35

Sunset Cemetery

501 South Franklin Street
Christiansburg, VA 24073

Sunset Cemetery, also known as Christiansburg Municipal Cemetery, was established in 1891, originally as a for-profit company in which the stockholders were paid with a free grave plot. In 1914, the cemetery became a nonprofit cemetery. In 2008, the Town of Christiansburg took ownership of the cemetery.[262]

The land where Sunset Cemetery resides has a long history. In 1808, a duel resulting in the death of two men took place here and led to duels being outlawed in Virginia.[263] Under the website's "Residents" section, visitors can read that there are many prominent citizens from Christiansburg who are buried here, yet they are not named. Only two individuals are named on the website. First, the cemetery highlights Charles T. Edie, who was buried in 1857 after he was killed by a fellow college student. The website points out that visitors can still see the inscription on his grave that reads, "Killed at Hampden-Sydney College Va." Second, the website states that "the most notorious resident buried at Sunset is Virginia Wardlaw, one of the murderous 'Black Sisters.' Wardlaw was accused in 1910 of murdering relatives for insurance money."[264]

Virginia Wardlaw, a woman who ran the Montgomery Female Academy in Christiansburg and was one of the notorious "Black Sisters," was known to come from a peculiar family. The sisters wore all black clothing and covered their faces with black veils. In 1910, Virginia Wardlaw, along with her sisters Caroline and Mary, was accused of murdering family members for insurance money.[265] Virginia Wardlaw starved herself to death before the judge in the

Sunset Cemetery, Christiansburg. *Author's collection.*

case could rule against her.[266] Wardlaw was buried in an unmarked grave in Sunset Cemetery.[267] People make pilgrimages to graves for various reasons, and this includes those following their interest in true crime. This is true for those interested in the bathtub tragedy that made headlines across the country and captivated readers' interest in the horrific crime. When visiting Sunset Cemetery, I saw that mementos were left at a broken grave within the family plot. Visitors have mistaken this as the destroyed marker of Virginia Wardlaw, who was buried in an unmarked grave, with the exact location of her burial never being included in the cemetery's records.[268] Even more eerie than seeing mementos left at the broken grave is realizing that the town's website emphasizes the darker events of history by listing the tragedies that occurred on the land and sharing an epitaph that notes a murder.

Just a few blocks away from the cemetery is the Montgomery Museum of Art & History. In 2018, the New River Stage performance of *Three Sisters Dressed in Black* was introduced by a museum docent, who offered the true story of the Wardlaw sisters. The museum also offers the Historic Christiansburg Walking Tour, which includes a visit to the location of the former Montgomery Female Academy, which was closed in 1908, after the sisters were suspected of having been involved with the deaths of family members.[269]

Today, the property where the school resided is considered to be haunted by the late sisters. Perhaps because of the sisters' association with cemeteries, Sunset Cemetery is also considered to be haunted by Virginia Wardlaw. As the legend states, the sisters would visit the cemetery at night. The wagon driver who took them to the cemetery witnessed the women performing rituals at a particular grave. Some say that a ghostly presence still visits the site. As the evening grows darker, drive by the cemetery to see if you can spot any specters. But be forewarned—do not enter the hallowed grounds after sunset. Worse than being followed home by something supernatural, a member of the Christiansburg Police Department may wish to take you to a much scarier place.

Speaking of scary places, the next stop on our tour gave me quite a fright when I was blocked on a trail after exiting the cemetery.

36

Pearis Cemetery

2030 Narrows Road
Narrows, VA 24124

I grew up in the country, but I should mention that I am more of a city cemetery visitor—think strolling down a well-worn path more than living off the land when it comes to nature! However, when I read that the Pearis Cemetery was right off the Appalachian Trail after a short hike, I looked forward to this adventure—and it was an undertaking!

The Pearis Cemetery trailhead is located near the intersection of Route 100/Narrows Road and Thomas Drive and close to the New River. There is a large sign and a gravel parking lot that can accommodate several vehicles.

Pearis Cemetery is the burial site of Captain George Pearis (1746–1810), a Revolutionary War soldier and the namesake of the town of Pearisburg. His memorial is a military-style headstone with a ground plaque enclosed by a brick wall. The cemetery includes a variety of memorials, including obelisks, traditional headstones and statuary that date from 1810 to 1930. The cemetery is secluded and haunted.

On July 22, 2024, I took the short hike that had two wooden benches along the trail. They gave me reassurance that I was heading in the right direction. The trail had had some gravel added at one point, but it was mostly dirt. Tree limbs and vines reached out to me as I walked the path. Having never hiked the Appalachian Trail, I was not sure what to expect. I did not see any other living souls on my way or within the cemetery. I was on high alert because of bears and snakes, but there have also been reports of shadowy apparitions, disembodied footsteps and even the sensation of being followed. I admit that I glanced behind me a few times as I made my way.

Above: Pearis Cemetery off the Appalachian Trail, Narrows. *Author's collection.*

Opposite, top: The memorial for Captain George Pearis, Narrows. *Author's collection.*

Opposite, bottom: The rustic stone bench at Pearis Cemetery off the Appalachian Trail, Narrows. *Author's collection.*

I arrived and walked up a short hill to see the clearing. Many of the markers have been broken, likely by environmental conditions, but overall, the cemetery is in good shape and appears to be well maintained, having had the grass cut somewhat recently before my visit and with new American flags on the military graves. The cemetery was larger than I had imagined, with nearly one hundred memorials. I was surprised by how ornate some of the markers were. Of course, some markers were in excellent condition and legible, while others had been weathered so much that they could not be read.

What struck me most was that I could not see Captain Pearis's brick enclosure or the large American flag until I walked through the cemetery. Even though there is a clearing, there are many large trees that obstruct the view. One large limb had broken from an even larger tree. There were some really interesting-looking headstones close to that tree, but I made sure to

CAPT.
GEO. PEARIS
VA. MIL.
REV. WAR

steer clear of any falling limbs or gravestones. After all, I was alone, and I'm mostly risk-averse.

Almost immediately, I saw a rustic stone bench that was positioned away from most of the grave markers. There was only one small headstone beside it. This was an eerie sight, but it was also strangely inviting. This was a place for visitors to rest and commune with the dead. I could not help but consider the folklore around mourning chairs, or haunted chairs as they're sometimes called. Stories associated with legend tripping, the adolescent practice of taking a nocturnal pilgrimage to places connected to urban legends, include superstitions about what would happen to the individual who dares to sit in these chairs or on these benches. If this cemetery was not so rural, I could imagine the stories teens would create for this bench. It turns out that there was another bench like this one, but being closer to an informational sign, it did not have the same uncanniness.

After spending time in the cemetery, I returned to the trail to head back, only to be blocked by a black rat snake that had zero interest in moving out of my way. I'm fairly frightened by snakes, but the alternative was me walking through poison ivy. I know that these snakes can be docile, and this one had kinked up its body and frozen as a defense, so I gently talked to him, telling him that he should carry on with his travels. He gave me a good ten-minute break to rest before he went on his way. In total, I think I walked through three spider webs and ended up with bugs all over me by the time I returned to my car. I had no experiences with ghosts, as I was pretty focused on not walking over a snake, but the visit was still amazing.

37

Pocahontas Cemetery

Pocahontas, VA 24635

When I talk about my grandfather, I am usually referring to my maternal grandfather, the genealogist. My father's father died from tuberculosis at the age of forty-four. My father was not quite ten years old as he watched his "Pop" live his final eighteen months in a sanitorium, where he could not hug his family. Stanley Pajka, my grandfather, had been a coal miner with the Susquehanna Coal Company in Luzerne, Pennsylvania, part of northern Appalachia. As I was heading to Tazewell County in southern Appalachia, I could not help but compare this part of Virginia with all my childhood trips to Pennsylvania traveling winding roads and steep inclines up mountains. The landscape was surprisingly similar. Visits to places near old coal mines were part of my childhood, but for this trip, I was headed to Pocahontas Cemetery, a cemetery that was established due to a coal mine disaster. On March 13, 1884, there was an explosion that claimed the lives of at least 114 miners in the Pocahontas East Mine. The bodies could not be recovered for a month, and when they were, they were interred here, in the town's first cemetery.

I cannot say that I have ever seen a cemetery like Pocahontas—and certainly not in Virginia. It's located on a steep hillside and has a variety of European-inspired funerary art, including symbols of the Russian Orthodox faith and an array of styles of gravestones like traditional headstones, obelisks, box tombs and mausoleums. In Pennsylvania, where my dad grew up, seeing Polish inscriptions on grave markers is somewhat common, but I haven't observed this in Virginia. In Pocahontas Cemetery, there are inscriptions in Polish, Russian, Italian, Hungarian and English. It is believed that coal

Left: The marker for Private Nicholaum Footo, Pocahontas Cemetery, Pocahontas. *Author's collection.*

Below: The memorial to the mining disaster of March 13, 1884. *Author's collection.*

barons went to Ellis Island to recruit immigrants to work in coal mines. This was not the American dream that they were promised.

One of my personal favorite memorials was a treestone-style marker that forms a crucifix; it belongs to George Marinyak, who was born, per his gravestone, in Austria-Hungary. Other memorials, including the marker for Private Nicholaum Footo (1896–1918), have a crucifix and an enameled portrait. It can be both unnerving and endearing looking at a portrait of someone on their grave. The inscription reads that he died "while serving in the medical corps with American expeditionary forces."

I was haunted by memories of my childhood and how my ancestors were connected to these Virginians; however, I had traveled here due to the legend of the miners who were buried in unmarked graves and continue to haunt the cemetery. Ghostly apparitions, disembodied sounds and strange feelings have been experienced by visitors.

In 2023, the town was awarded $140,000 in state funds for the restoration of the cemetery, which will be overseen by the Virginia Department of Historic Resources.[270] Part of the funding will be used for ground-penetrating radar to locate graves. Perhaps the ghosts of the miners and their families are curious about the renovation efforts and all the investment of time and funding put into their final resting place.

Down the hill, toward the historical marker that is on Centre Street, near the intersection of Pocahontas Avenue and Falls Mills Road, Historic Pocahontas Inc., a nonprofit organization working to preserve the history and landmarks in the town, added a marker on the one hundredth anniversary of the disaster. The marker reads, "Erected in Memory of 114 Coal Miners Killed in the East Mine of the Southwest Virginia Improvement CO. March 13, 1884." Annually, the nonprofit holds a candlelight vigil in honor of the miners who were lost to the disaster.[271] The town members do not let the memory of these miners fade, so I imagine the ghosts are there to stay.

Heading out from the cemetery that was built because of a mining disaster, our next stop is an illuminating look at a ghost in Bluefield.

EERIE EXTRA: MAPLE HILL CEMETERY

BLUEFIELD, VA 24605

In a 1930 article of *The Roanoke Times*, the headline reads "Bluefield 'Ghost' to Trouble No More."[272] The reporter explains, "For the past year the

Above: Maple Hill Cemetery, Bluefield. *Author's collection.*

Left: The Roanoke Times, *September 19, 1930.*

BLUEFIELD "GHOST" TO TROUBLE NO MORE

Bluefield, Va., Sept. 18 (Special).—

report of a mysterious light in Maple Hill cemetery at night has been widely advertised with the result that many persons have been visiting the cemetery lane at night in automobiles."[273] Those who were living near the cemetery were "greatly annoyed as the result of the 'ghost' in the cemetery." At first, the situation was treated like a joke, but once local police officers verified "the presence of the light," they set out to determine the source.

The results of the investigation are not so spooky. Citizens "claimed the phenomenon was caused by the reflection of a street [light] on a tomb stone." The Appalachian Power Company, after numerous complaints, agreed "to remove the cemetery 'ghost.'" The light was removed, and the ghost did not return.

I visited Maple Hill Cemetery on July 22, 2024. It is a lovely cemetery with a super steep drive around the perimeter of the grounds. If you are at all afraid of heights, this cemetery might be a bit too spooky for you.

38

Sinking Spring Cemetery

Russell Road Northwest
Abingdon, VA 24210

Our next spooky cemetery is located seventy-six miles south of Bluefield in the Town of Abingdon, which was originally called Wolf Hills. The local lore is that pioneer and folk hero Daniel Boone had his dogs attacked here by a pack of wolves in the 1760s, and that is how the town's name originated. Several businesses still use the name Wolf Hills. It sets the tone for this next haunted cemetery—Sinking Spring Cemetery.

The cemetery was intended for members of the Sinking Spring Presbyterian Church, which was organized in 1773 and led by Reverend Charles Cummings. The earliest marked grave is from 1776. Pioneers, citizens and veterans of the Revolutionary War, the War of 1812 and the Civil War make up the approximate three thousand interments.

I visited Sinking Spring Cemetery on July 23, 2024. From my hotel, I stopped by the visitors' center to pick up a map and brochure of the cemetery before walking over to the grounds. There were historical signs and other informational signs at the entrance, including one that reads, "All burials must be pre authorized [*sic*]." That was an interesting warning before entering.

One of the first features in the cemetery that I noticed was a log cabin with a sign that read, "The Parsons Cummings Cabin Circa 1773." The earliest meetinghouse was constructed out of logs on this land. The log manse seen today was moved to this location from its original location north of the cemetery in 1971.

The mound at Sinking Spring Cemetery, Abingdon. *Author's collection.*

There are many styles of memorials, including obelisks, slant markers, treestone monuments, cradle graves, traditional headstones and statues of angels. I even spotted one zinc obelisk, also known as a bluestone, marketed as white bronze. These were the more affordable option from the 1870s to the 1910s, and they have outlasted many stone markers. I also noticed that many of the gravestones include insignias of Masons and Oddfellows.

When I was doing research about the hauntings, I discovered that one of the people buried here, Judge Robert William Hughes, was an acquaintance of the writer Edgar Allan Poe. The inscription on his large obelisk reads, "Journalist. Author. Jurist."

Before arriving, I was anxious about finding "The Mound" because this is where many of the cemetery hauntings are said to take place; however, not only is it located on the map in the brochure, but I could also see the large grass- and ivy-covered tomb when I first drove by the cemetery the day before. This is where a ghost of a young girl haunts.

With reports of glowing orbs; movement from the iron door to the tomb, which opens and closes without any human assistance; and whispers having been reported coming from around the crypt, this was one spooky memorial to visit.[274] It was uncanny. I had not seen anything quite like it, and it certainly stands out in this cemetery. What I would not have known after a mere glimpse is that the mound covers a stone tomb similar to the way a bunker mausoleum is placed into the side of a hill. The iron bars enclose the tomb and a grave marker to John Henry Martin (1824–1899) and his wife, Malinda Martin (1819–1893). The local lore is that John Henry Martin wished to be buried while standing upright.

Several people in town mentioned in the most scandalous way how many wives John Henry Martin had; however, walking through the cemetery, it was the grave of John A. Hagy (1828–1904) and the two graves next to his, those of Sarah A., the wife of John A. Hagy (1824–1891), and B. Emeline, the wife of John A. Hagy (1830–1868), that stood out to me. From the inscriptions on the graves and the death dates, it appears that John A. Hagy, who outlived both of his wives, was buried next to his second wife, Sarah, who was buried between John and his first wife, Emeline. When I'm giving tours, I often point out how size matters when it comes to grave markers, especially focusing on wealth and esteem. And in this case, even though Sarah ended up between her husband and his first wife, her marker is shorter and smaller in size. I am reading into these stones without knowing any of their stories. Let this be a reminder to each of us to be both perceptive and nonjudgmental when wandering these sacred grounds so nothing comes back to haunt us.

39

EAST HILL CEMETERY

STATE STREET
BRISTOL, VA 24201

This next haunted cemetery is one for the books—literally! Everything I have learned about the ghosts in East Hill Cemetery has come from articles or books that all lead back to one man. I never met Victor N. "Bud" Phillips (1929–2017) when he was alive, but his writing and storytelling have changed me. And from what I have read, it changed Bristol, too. His writing blends history and contemporary ghost sightings.

Bud Phillips came to Bristol in 1953, and he became one of the "best known citizens," per the erected historical sign placed within the cemetery. One of the cemetery roads is named after him, and there has even been a "Bud Phillips Day" that was recognized in Bristol on May 5. He became the official historian, wrote several local history books and a popular newspaper column, had two television shows and a radio show and was a tour guide. I share this because while I was excited to tour a haunted cemetery, I wanted to visit Bud's grave to pay my respects in the very cemetery where he told stories. It's historians like Bud Phillips who pass along a region's history to the next generation. I'm excited to share that many of these stories are spooky!

I first read the article "East Hill Cemetery Is the Most Haunted Place in the City of Bristol" in the *Bristol Herald Courier*.[275] In the piece, authored by Phillips, he shares ghostly tales of the land that would become the cemetery. He weaves in history with his storytelling, sharing that Nellie Gaines, age five, was the first person to be buried here, and this was the start of the cemetery. Not long after, two other little girls were buried in the cemetery; then came reports of ghost lights and the sounds of giggles.

East Hill Cemetery is the most haunted place in the city of Bristol

Top: The marker for "Bud" Phillips, East Hill Cemetery, Bristol. *Author's collection.*

Bottom: Bristol Herald Courier, *December 29, 2013.*

Phillips also included a story of a woman who was searching for her great-grandmother's grave in the cemetery and having a difficult time locating it. As dusk was nearing, she was ready to abandon her search, but she felt an urge to look one more time when she discovered that she was not alone in the cemetery. There was "a tall gray-haired lady standing beside a low shrub." The lady was wearing a long pale pink dress and appeared to be beckoning to the woman. "This lady kept pointing downward toward that shrub," and then the lady disappeared. The woman who had been searching moved to the area where the tall lady had been standing. Looking down, she found her great-grandmother's grave. She realized that the figure had been wearing a dress that she recalled being told her great-grandmother had been buried in. She shared with Phillips "that she firmly believed she had finally been able to see her relative."[276]

Of course, many others have worked to keep East Hill Cemetery's ghost stories alive and well. Annually, there is the East Hill Cemetery Ghost Walk near the end of October. Actors in period clothing share tales of those from Bristol's past. The goal is to teach history and encourage interest in the cemetery; however, the actors acknowledge that things that happen in the cemetery cannot always be explained, and their ghost walk trickles in these ghostly tales.[277]

One story they share is of the ghostly drummer boy whose drumbeat can still be heard near the graves of Civil War soldiers. East Hill Cemetery includes more than one hundred graves in the Confederate section. One of those unmarked graves belongs to the young boy from Georgia who lied about his age in order to join the war efforts. He traveled with the company for months, but like so many soldiers during that time, he became ill with a fever. He was sent to a local hospital. One of Bristol's local women known for her kindness went to visit him; he mistook her for his own mother, and he asked to be taken home. She could not refuse his final wishes and brought the boy to her home. Eventually, he passed away from the illness. Although most fallen soldiers were buried hastily, the community members purchased a nice coffin for the boy and had flowers for his burial. He was buried in the western slope.

Bristol's annual memorial service included a recognition for the fallen soldiers. In the early 1900s, one speaker told a story about the Georgia drummer boy, and during the speech, those in attendance could hear the faint sound of a drumbeat. While some members of the community were frightened enough to leave the cemetery, Major Henry C. Wood and other veterans remained. "They knew that they were hearing a sound from Civil War days repeated after the passage of nearly forty years. They considered this to be almost a spiritual occurrence." Community members have heard the faint drumbeats from time to time.[278]

There is also the tale about a young girl named Sally, who left home and secretly married a man named Milton without her family knowing. Her father looked for her all over town when he learned of her nuptials. Angered that his daughter had run around behind his back, he looked for her for weeks. Finally, he saw his daughter and her new husband. He stopped what he was doing and set out after the couple, raising his pistol to the young husband. He fired, but it was his daughter who jumped in front of the bullet

The grave of Revolutionary War General Evan Shelby East Hill Cemetery, Bristol. *Author's collection.*

in order to protect her love. Sally died almost instantly, and the father shot Milton in the heart.

Both were buried in the cemetery but in very different areas. She was interred a lot farther up the hillside, while the young husband was buried in the paupers' section in the lower part of the cemetery. As the legend shares, witnesses have seen shimmering lights rising from both of their graves. The lights head toward each other. Townsfolks call these mysterious lights "ghost-courting lights" of the young Sally and her husband, Milton.[279]

I visited East Hill Cemetery on July 23, 2024. The cemetery has some gorgeous markers, including treestone graves with stone floral hanging baskets, obelisks, angels, cherubs and some larger white bronze markers. One of my favorite gravestones is that of Revolutionary War General Evan

Shelby (1719–1794), who was born in Wales. He became a North Carolina state senator, was a brigadier general of militia and declined to become governor of the lost state of Franklin in 1787. General Shelby's gravestone is in the shape of a coffin. There is a military marker at the head of the grave and a plaque that was placed by the General Evan Shelby Chapter NSDAR of Kentucky on the one hundredth anniversary of the chapter's formation, October 12, 1997.

Of course, I also visited Bud Phillips's grave, which includes a bench with the inscription, "Friend rest here a while and look to the west and view the city which I chose for my home in 1953 and found it to be truly a good place to live." I sat on the bench. I looked out at the city. I promise you, the warm feeling that I experienced was not merely the sun.

EERIE EXTRA: ONE GHOST WALK IN TWO STATES!

In Bristol, you can be in two places at once! The annual ghost walk tour includes portions of two states, because East Hill Cemetery crosses the state line between Bristol, Virginia, and Bristol, Tennessee. Visit the iconic State Street in Historic Downtown, which is the line between the states.

Proving that I'm often on the wrong side of the tracks. The Bristol sign separating Virginia and Tennessee. *Author's collection.*

40

Laurel Grove Cemetery

4812–4850 VA-74
Norton, VA 24273

Sixty-four miles northwest of Bristol is Laurel Grove Cemetery, also called Laurel Grove Cemetery at Ramsey or Ramsey Cemetery. The cemetery is located in Norton, an independent city in Wise County. There are over five thousand interments in the cemetery. One of the oldest marked graves is that of Reverend Thomas Easterling, noted as a soldier in the Revolutionary War who died in 1815. Many of the graves date to the mid-1800s and continue today, since this is an active cemetery.

The area was mountainous, and the roads within the cemetery grounds were winding. I had an eerie feeling at first. This cemetery is haunted; visitors have felt temperatures drop to become surprisingly chilly on hot days, and there have been sightings of shadowy figures and even the movement of leaves or small flags when there was not even a breeze. I pulled in the cemetery and immediately stopped to look at a large rectangular marker with a crucifix on top. The grave belongs to Juily Maiolo, who passed at just five years old. I was taken by the beauty of the marker, but again, there was an eeriness to the cemetery. I swore that I heard something like a low buzzing. One of the hauntings that has been shared is the sound of disembodied voices. This sound did not resemble speaking. I thought I remembered reading something about people hearing a train in the middle of the cemetery. This was different. Fortunately, I paid attention to that sound before walking up to the Maiolo marker, because it had a large, almost heart-shaped, shaggy casing that hung under the right side of the crucifix under stone Jesus's left arm. It was a bald-faced hornets' nest, and they can be aggressive. I backed

Above: The entrance to Laurel Grove Cemetery, with the grave of Dock Boggs visible in the background, Norton. *Author's collection.*

Left: A hornets' nest in Laurel Grovc Cemetery, Norton. *Author's collection.*

up slowly to my car. I had encountered two bees' nests on my journeys of Virginia's haunted cemeteries, but this was my first hornets' nest, and it was scary. I was not in much of a mood to look at graves outside of my car at that point.

There was one grave that I wanted to visit though. I made a point to find the grave of Dock Boggs (February 7, 1898–February 7, 1971), an old-time singer, songwriter and banjo player who played Appalachian folk music and Black American blues. Boggs is buried beside his wife, Sarah, in a grave near the entrance of the cemetery on the right side. The gravestone is a rectangular granite marker with two separate enameled portraits of Boggs and his wife. The epitaph reads, "Rest Sweet Rest."

Boggs's music was included in *The Anthology of American Folk Music*, edited by Harry Smith (1923–1991) and considered one of the most influential releases in the history of recorded sound. There are several songs archived on YouTube. I recommend listening to "Oh Death," a traditional Appalachian folk song, which can be found on the Smithsonian Folk Ways Recordings.[280]

The children prayed, the preacher preached
Time and mercy is out of your reach
I'll fix your feet 'til you can't walk
I'll lock your jaw 'til you can't talk
I'll close your eyes so you can't see
This very hour, come and go with me
I'm death I come to take the soul
Leave the body and leave it cold
To draw up the flesh off of the frame
Dirt and worm both have a claim
O, Death
O, Death
Won't you spare me over 'til another year[281]

The Ominous End

With haunted cemeteries on haunted college campuses, a spooky cemetery off the Appalachian Trail, true crime and the grave of a local legend, the haunting stories from the Blue Rudge and Southwest Virginia stayed with me even after my journey home. I immediately attended the Unhallowed Grounds National Tour, a staged storytelling like the old-time radio plays hosted by the horror podcast *Old Gods of Appalachia.* I just cannot get enough of this region. Alas, this tour of haunted cemeteries takes us to one more region, and I promise it's a good one, filled with more Civil War soldiers, true crime and even a documented case of a woman being buried alive. Gather your nerves! We're heading to the Shenandoah Valley.

Part V
Shenandoah Valley

The Shenandoah Valley is part of the Great Appalachian Valley, a massive trough that includes a chain of valley lowlands. In this region, I'll share stories from some of the region's independent cities, as well as the counties. This is a region that offers scenic trails and unique experiences. It also has some haunted cemeteries with stories that are *deeply* frightening. Let's move to our first eerie location.

41
Oak Grove Cemetery

316 South Main Street
Lexington, VA 24450

Oak Grove Cemetery is located less than a mile from the Virginia Military Institute campus. The cemetery was previously known as Presbyterian Cemetery and was renamed Stonewall Jackson Memorial Cemetery in 1863 to honor the Confederate general. In 2020, the cemetery was renamed once again.

Oak Grove Cemetery, Lexington. *Author's collection.*

This cemetery haunts me; it is the third time it has shown up in my research. The first time I visited was to see the grave of author and poet Margaret Junkin Preston, who was considered a southern war poet. My second visit to the cemetery was to see the grave of her husband, John T.L. Preston, who was childhood friends with the writer Edgar Allan Poe.

Buried here are a war general and 144 veterans of the Civil War, including many who were killed in Manassas and Chancellorsville; it is not a surprise that people call this old cemetery haunted. This is a popular and convenient stop for ghost tours to visit, as it is right off South Main Street. Ghostly sightings include apparitions of soldiers walking through the cemetery and even stories about Southern generals and their ghost horses riding down the streets. If, however, you glimpse a soldier seemingly floating among the trees in the center of the cemetery, that is not an apparition but the statue of General Thomas "Stonewall" Jackson (1824–1863), sculpted by Edward Virginius Valentine of Richmond and erected in 1891.

A booklet, *Walking Tour through Oak Grove Cemetery*, by the Historic Lexington Foundation, is available in a box at the cemetery's entrance. The cemetery is open from dawn to dusk, although I caution any late evening visitors, as it appears Lexington is an extremely haunted place.

42

CEDAR HILL CEMETERY

COVINGTON, VA

Taking an approximately forty-mile trip west from Lexington brings us to Cedar Hill Cemetery, a sixty-acre historic cemetery with grave markers dating to 1816. The cemetery is owned and operated by the City of Covington. Many types of grave markers can be found among the ten thousand memorials, including military markers for veterans from the Civil War, the Spanish-American War, World War I, World War II, the Korean War and the Vietnam War.[282] With Cedar Hill's large number of interments, it is not surprising that it is connected to a legend from the Alleghany Highlands, along with numerous ghost sightings like blue lights that appear over graves.

In an article from July 2, 1930, in *The Covington Virginian*, the reporter shares an odd occurrence in Cedar Hill Cemetery.

> *When one man sees a ghost in a graveyard, something is wrong with him, but when four boys see it together and others see the same thing later, something is wrong with the graveyard.*
>
> *And something sure seems to be wrong in the Cedar Hill Cemetery. Queer lights are dancing around out there. That is, they dance until someone approaches them and then they just pass away.*[283]

The article shares that a boy on a bus with several passengers first saw the light close to midnight. The driver pulled over, and he, along with a few passengers, went out to investigate what was making the dancing light in the

CLAIM GHOST SEEN IN CEDAR HILL CEMETERY

Blue Light Appears Dancing Over Graves

Left: Covington Virginian, *July 2, 1930.*

Below: The grave of Annie Jeter, Cedar Hill Cemetery Covington. *Author's collection.*

cemetery. "Their description of it makes it seem as if it were a flame of some nature, almost bluish in color and dancing around always over the same lot but never in the same place."[284] The group walked toward the spot of the light and could not find anything that could have produced the flame. They "left in a hurry."[285]

Around 3:00 a.m. that same night, another driver passing the cemetery saw the light, and a woman who was taking a sick husband to the doctor happened to see the light and reported it.[286] While several reports came in and people went out to the cemetery the following nights, I could not find any follow-up reports to resolve the mystery.

Another local legend is that of the ghost of Mrs. Jeter, which is connected to an actual grave in the cemetery, that of Annie Jeter (1864–1912) and her husband, James Garrett Jeter (1860–1938). The legend states that the Jeter statue, which depicts a woman walking down three steps, comes directly from the scene of their wedding day, when, while walking down the church steps, Mrs. Jeter fell and broke her neck. Annie Jeter lived into her late forties and had children, so the legend is not a true account of the woman for whom the memorial was erected.

Other eerie tales include one that says the statue trickles blood, but only on one night a year—Halloween. News reporters have gone out on October 31 to try to witness these events to no avail.[287]

SPOOKY SPECIAL

In folklore, blue fire or blue flames are associated with supernatural or mystical phenomena. For example, in Slavic folklore, blue flames were linked to supernatural creatures or events. In the novel *Dracula* (1897) by Bram Stoker, Jonathan Harker rides in a carriage on his way to meet his host and notices eerie blue flames appearing in the mountains. When he later asks Dracula about this, he is told that on St. George's Eve, the flames indicate buried treasure. Wills-o'-the-wisp, or ghost lights, are often attributed to ghosts or spirits. Science explains the lights as natural phenomena, such as bioluminescence or chemiluminescence caused by oxidation produced by organic decay.

EERIE EXTRA: BURIED ALIVE!

In *The Ghosts of Virginia*, a story about a Covington woman who was buried alive gives readers chills. The author shares that an editor of *The Virginian Review* wrote a special issue in 1997 that shared the story of a young wife, Martha Jordan, who gave birth to her baby Lucy Ira Jordan. The baby died within a couple of months, and the aggrieved mother was thought to have passed on February 28, 1848. A Works Progress Administration writer in 1937 reported that after forty years of burial, the Jordan graves were to be moved to another part of the cemetery, and new caskets would be necessary. "The undertaker found that Martha Jordan had turned over on her face and her hand was up at her head. This is the only known occasion of anyone in this county being buried alive." It is speculated that she had some type of seizure and was in coma at the time that she was buried.[288]

> *The fear of being buried alive is perhaps as old as the fear of death itself. Being taken from this world at the moment of death is bad enough, but the prospect of being mistakenly identified as dead and then waiting in suffocating horror…well, it's too much for most of us to think about.*[289]

A recent article in *The Virginian Review* focuses on the two stories and adds that Martha Jordan and her daughter's memorial are near the Jeter statue, which could be the origin of the Mrs. Jeter ghost story.[290] The reporter describes the Jordan grave marker as being "shaped like a keyhole."[291]

On August 7, 2024, I visited the cemetery. As I drove up the one-way entrance, I immediately spotted the Jordan memorial, thanks to a distinctive treestone nearby. I drove by the open field with monuments dotting the landscape to my right in the oldest section of the cemetery, section I, and a similar view to my left, section II. I parked under some trees for shade and to make sure other cars could pass by me. While parking, I could see the Jeter statue on the corner to the left of the road. It is hard to miss.

Cedar Hill Cemetery is a lovely old cemetery that is still active, meaning that burials still occur there. As I was meandering through the oldest area, several cars and a funeral procession passed by.

"The Premature Burial," by Edgar A Poe, was published in 1844, and here I was visiting the grave of a woman who was buried alive on my birthday in 1848. This was during a time when security coffins were built to include ropes to ring bells, air tubes and escape levers to assist the unfortunate individual who had been buried alive. Absolutely nothing frightens me more, and yet Jordan's grave isn't even the one that is considered haunted in this cemetery.

An article from *The Abingdon Virginian* in 1868 shares, "A Mr. Frank Vesley, of Newark, has invented a patent safety coffin," and it says that the inventor, so confident in his creation, would demonstrate the device by being buried in it, and "he proposes to resurrect himself and to come forth unaided and uninjured."[292]

SPOOKY SPECIAL

Live burial remains the most awful fate imaginable. Not because it is especially likely. Not even because of the grisly details. But because it disrupts our fond dreaming of an ordered world, in which death and life are cleanly separated by six feet of earth.[293]

OF COURSE, THIS COULD not happen today, right? Our society is much too orderly. It's best not to contemplate on these thoughts for too long, but I recall reading about the woman who woke up in a Polish morgue in 2009 and an Australian man who had to escape his own body bag in 2022.[294]

43
Thornrose Cemetery

1041 West Beverley Street
Staunton, VA 24401

Heading back toward Lexington and traveling forty miles north, our next tour stop is Thornrose Cemetery in Staunton, "one of the most historic and visually stunning facilities of its kind in the nation."[295] The cemetery was chartered in 1849, with twelve acres laid out in lots, roads and walkways. The cemetery was formally dedicated on May 28, 1853, with its first burial taking place the next day. The cemetery later expanded to comprise thirty acres and added a limestone gatehouse, a bridge and tower, a chapel and a stone wall to enclose it.

I first visited Thornrose Cemetery on April 7, 2021, to see the grave of Eva Howard Clark (1881–1906), a trapeze artist with the Cole Brothers Circus in the early twentieth century. Staunton was on the circuit, and the Cole Brother Circus was in business from 1844 to 2016. Each time a circus came to town, performers would pay Eva Clark's gravesite a visit and decorate her grave with flowers. After her death in 1906, this was the only marking for her grave until 1923, when "friends with Hagenbeck-Wallace Circus" erected an official grave marker.[296]

Local lore connected to Clark's grave shares that each Christmas, a mysterious visitor leaves a wreath on her grave. But this visitor has never been identified. To me, that is more endearing than spooky. But once upon a time, Thornrose Cemetery did have a "ghost."

In September 1951, locals were concerned about the "eerie noises" and "fleeting swishes through the foliage" that were heard and seen in the cemetery. Without a clear explanation, residents wondered if the cemetery

Cemetery Ghost Turns
Out To Be Just Monkey

STAUNTON, Sept. 20 (AP)—

Top: The Roanoke Times, *September 21, 1951.*

Bottom: The grave of trapeze artist Eva Howard Clark in Thornrose Cemetery, Staunton. *Author's collection.*

was haunted. Could this be a ghost? Nope. It turns out that it was only a monkey. "Nobody could explain how the monkey—about the size of a cat—got to Staunton....But all were glad the cemetery is as quiet again as it should be."[297] There were speculations that the monkey had been someone's pet or even an escapee from a local circus. Had there actually been a ghost in Thornrose Cemetery, the locals would have gone bananas!

Entering the cemetery through a stone arch and gatehouse that was designed by local architect T.J. Collins and built by William Larner &

Company, visitors will see the footbridge and tower. The cemetery includes a row of mausoleums that is often referred to as the "city of the dead." Other than the impressive collection of mortuary art, I was taken by how it appeared that every grave faced east. While this is a tradition in Christian burial grounds, the graves in Thornrose Cemetery add a bit of drama. I had to go to the eastern part of the cemetery to see anything other than the backs of graves. Before meandering, I searched for Eva Howard Clark's grave, located in section 10.

I do not recall which true crime piece I first read that introduced me to Eva Clark, a victim of a violent death, but a biographical sketch in 2020 encouraged my visit to her grave.

Áine Murphy Norris wrote, "[Clark's] biography [is] a narrative that must shift to focus on the performer's life and career, and not only her tragic death."[298] Unfortunately, stories like Clark's that end up being retold "through ghost tours, regional storytelling, and dramatized narratives [become] caught in the space between an incomplete reality and local lore. However, it is that local lore that has kept their story alive."[299] If you're taking a ghost tour in Staunton, just be sure to have your peanuts and popcorn ready for the embellished storytelling. Then stop by Clark's grave and leave her a little token.

44

Saint Michael's Church Cemetery

9803 Saint Michaels Lane
Bridgewater, VA 22812

Seventeen miles north of Thornrose Cemetery is Saint Michael's Church Cemetery. Of the over 350 burials in the churchyard, one of the oldest graves marks where Reverand Benjamin Henkel (1765–1794) was buried under the chancel of the old church. There are gravestones denoting those who served in the military, including during the Civil War.

The cemetery is surrounded by fields dotted with trees with mountains in the background. When I visited on October 4, 2024, there was a fog warning in the area. It was as thick as clouds and nearly covered the pond behind the churchyard; a weeping willow tree emerged from the mist, creating the perfect atmosphere for my visit. If one was walking up that hill toward the church, they would see Saint Michael's in the background and the grave of Private Adam W. Kersh (1828–1905) just before them. Kersh's grave is a white marble marker that resembles a podium with the shape of a book resting on the top. Kersh's ghost does not give a lecture though; that would be out of character for him. Instead, it is said that "on breezing nights you can see him sit on his tombstone while he plays his fiddle."[300]

What I enjoy about this ghost story is that the apparition is connected to a real person who lived and died in the area. On July 31, 1861, after failing to find a paid substitute to replace him, Kersh enlisted in Company F, Virginia Fifty-Second Infantry Regiment, where he remained until the end of the Civil War. His letters to his brother, George P. Kersh, document his experiences during the war and his good fortune that he was able to send

Saint Michael's Church Cemetery, Bridgewater. *Author's collection.*

The grave of Private Adam W. Kersh. *Author's collection.*

and receive letters. His correspondence also notes that he was well known by his fellow soldiers for his ability to play the fiddle.[301]

After the war, Kersh returned to his real life, where he had a profession as a cabinet- and chair-maker, although archaeological evidence from his workshop shows that he was repairing or making fiddles as well.[302]

45

STRASBURG PRESBYTERIAN CHURCH AND CEMETERY

325 SOUTH HOLLIDAY STREET
STRASBURG, VA 22657

Nearly eighty miles north of Staunton is the Strasburg Presbyterian Church, a historic Presbyterian church that was built in 1830 in Shenandoah County. German-speaking Pennsylvanians settled in this area and built their family farms.

Strasburg Presbyterian Church is the oldest building still standing in Strasburg. The churchyard is located on the eastern side of the sanctuary. The churchyard includes burials from the Civil War and those of veterans

Riverview Cemetery is located behind Strasburg Presbyterian Church and Cemetery, Strasburg. *Author's collection.*

from the War of 1812. Behind the churchyard is a much larger cemetery, Riverview Cemetery, also called Strasburg Cemetery. Walking back behind the churchyard into Riverview Cemetery, I saw breathtaking views of the mountains. What a gorgeous place to spend eternity.

The haunting label attached to the churchyard came after the church served as a hospital to both Confederate and Union troops during the Civil War. Reports of ghosts of Confederate soldiers walking the cemetery grounds and the nearby road have been shared. A twenty-foot-tall obelisk in the churchyard marks the final resting place of 136 Confederate soldiers. Perhaps some of these soldiers never left this part of Strasburg.

46

OLD QUEEN STREET GRAVEYARD

339 QUEEN STREET
STRASBURG, VA 22657

A half mile from the Strasburg Presbyterian Church is the cemetery known as the Old Graveyard, the Old Queen Street Graveyard and even the Old Indian Graveyard. The cemetery is located next to Mt. Zion United Methodist Church. It has no clear ownership, although the town takes care of the property.

This is Strasburg's oldest public cemetery with the oldest surviving headstones, and it is rumored that the town's founder, Peter Stover, was buried here. The graveyard comprises a half acre and includes some of the region's oldest family names.

On the Strasburg Virginia Heritage Association Ghost Tour, the guide mentions Brother Obadiah Samuel Funk, a member of the Ephrata Cloister and the Christian Order of Ephrata. Ephrata Cloister was a religious community or commune established in 1732 in what is now known as Lancaster County, Pennsylvania. "Sabbatarians," as they were called, leaned toward spiritual mysticism. Members had positive outlooks on life and enjoyed respecting their neighbors and the environment. They were famous for writing and publishing hymns, and in Strasburg, they played a significant role in introducing pottery to the community.

The cemetery includes interments from the Civil War. With the cemetery's location right off the road and it being surrounded by trees, it's no surprise that stories mention the faint images of ghostly Confederate soldiers being seen in the cemetery and down Queen Street.

Old Queen Street Graveyard, Strasburg. *Author's collection.*

EERIE EXTRA: ST. PAUL'S LUTHERAN CHURCH CEMETERY

156 WEST WASHINGTON STREET
STRASBURG, VA 22657

This cemetery is a half mile from Old Queen Street Graveyard and has a fascinating story, because there are so many unknowns. When was the church first built? Who built the church in this location? The first records date from 1769. Although the church was dilapidated before the Civil War, Union soldiers gutted the building and used it as a hospital, arsenal and even a stable for their horses.[303] The bell tower and Neo-Gothic aesthetic were added in 1893, and the church was renovated again in 1986.

I visited the cemetery on June 12, 2024. The road is much lower than the cemetery grounds, which sit on a hill surrounded by a stone wall. The cemetery includes a variety of gravestones. It almost feels like they're glaring down—not that the graveyard seems ominous. The grass is well maintained, as are the memorials. It is just the position of the sidewalk

St. Paul's Lutheran Church Cemetery, Strasburg. *Author's collection.*

being lower or actually level with the graves that makes it feel like I, too, am buried and looking up out of the ground. Eek! This would be a good time for a ghost story.

This ghost story connects to those who are buried in the cemetery and continue to haunt their old home that is two blocks away. For this story, we head to the Balzer Huber House (148 West Queen Street), which is on the Strasburg Ghost Tour. The house was originally built in 1765 as a log cabin. The house has been haunted for centuries by a couple who lived there in the 1800s. Ghostly encounters have included the smell of a distinct perfume when no one alive is wearing such a scent and even sightings of a woman in period clothing walking the property. The male apparition has also been sighted, and he comes with the smell of cigars.[304] According to one of the owners of the house, the ghostly couple included a woman who married a man beneath her social status and was disowned by her family. The unnamed couple—a fact that unfortunately makes their story hard to corroborate—are buried in unmarked graves at St. Paul's Cemetery.[305]

47
Prospect Hill Cemetery

200 West Prospect Street
Front Royal, VA 22630

Traveling east of Strasburg, I reached Prospect Hill Cemetery in Front Royal on the afternoon of June 12, 2024. My initial fright was that the road to the main entrance was closed for construction, and I could not find another way to enter the cemetery. Fortunately, I found a paved alley that let me access the entrance. Today, the cemetery covers approximately forty-two acres and holds over eleven thousand burials. On the day I visited, the cemetery appeared well maintained, with its grass recently cut. (Although a gopher was wreaking havoc on one old grave.)

Although the oldest grave dates to 1802, many families have reinterred their loved ones at Prospect Hill. The cemetery association was granted a charter in 1872.[306] The history goes back to the Civil War. This location is where General Stonewall Jackson's troops took their first look at Front Royal on May 23, 1862.

Like Sharon Cemetery in Northern Virginia, Prospect Hill also has a circular soldiers' memorial to its Confederate dead. In 1868, the Ladies Warren Memorial Society initiated the gathering of the soldiers' remains to be interred at Prospect Hill. The unveiling of the monument occurred in June 1882.[307] The memorial includes the remains of 90 soldiers who were identifiable, and those of 186 unidentified soldiers are interred in the middle of the circle. The soldiers are from all states of the Confederacy.[308]

Like with so many of the cemeteries connected to the Civil War, I was not surprised to learn that one of the ghosts in Prospect Hill Cemetery has been seen kneeling at a grave in Soldiers' Circle. The apparition appears in military attire and weeps or appears saddened over a grave. Perhaps the

Prospect Hill Cemetery, Front Royal. *Author's collection.*

spirit is realizing that this is his grave and that he died in the war. I did not see any other visitors during my visit, and it was easy to have my eyes play tricks on me with a variety of obelisks and column grave markers. What struck me as odd as I walked around the Soldiers' Circle is that I smelled something burning, as if someone had set a campfire within the grounds of the cemetery. The day was quite warm, so I could not imagine that any of the local homes had their stoves burning. Was this some phantom smell, also known as phantosmia? Or was there actually something burning nearby? It did, however, set the tone for my visit, as I meandered through old gravestones and peeped into a nearby mausoleum. It was there that I believed I might have seen the other ghost that haunts the cemetery—a grieving woman dressed in nineteenth-century clothing. (I have read that it was specifically 1880s clothing. That seems terribly specific, and I assume whoever saw the apparition was familiar with the natural form and second bustle periods—I certainly cannot differentiate the styles of the 1870s and 1880s.) Perhaps the ghost simply has a protruding backside, mimicking a shelf bustle, or perhaps it was just the shadows playing tricks. I heard no one crying, and again, I saw no other souls in the cemetery. But there was that burning scent that lingered. That would remain a mystery as the sun slowly set and the cemetery gates closed for the day.

48

Mount Hebron Cemetery

305 East Boscawen Street
Winchester, VA 22601

A little over twenty miles from Front Royal, the last cemetery on our tour is Mount Hebron Cemetery, which is four burying grounds enclosed together. The oldest section that is believed to have been a burying place for two centuries is the section in the northwest corner. This cemetery once surrounded the Reformed church and covers just over an acre. Graves there date to 1769. Next to this section is the Lutheran Cemetery, which also covers over an acre. This is north of the entranceway. This section includes gravestones with skulls and crossbones. The oldest marked grave dates to 1777. Mount Hebron Cemetery was added to the burying grounds in 1844. It originally comprised five acres and now extends to fifty-six. The last burying ground within the Mount Hebron Cemetery complex was dedicated in 1866, and it is certainly the most haunted.

Stonewall Cemetery is the resting place for 2,576 Confederate soldiers.[309] This cemetery includes graves of soldiers who are grouped by state, with a monument to the unknown soldiers in the middle. The entire cemetery complex was enclosed with an iron fence in 1891. In 1902, the limestone tower gate, which was the gate keeper's residence, as well as office space, was added.

Mount Hebron Cemetery has an impressive entrance. Visitors can walk or drive under the tower gate. There is parking available within the cemetery, near the offices, and visitors can drive through the cemetery, although I encourage everyone who can to get out of the car and traverse the grounds.

The grave of the Patton brothers, Stonewall Cemetery in Mount Hebron, Winchester. *Author's collection.*

Of course, with a cemetery that contains so many burials from war, it can't be a surprise that there are ghost stories about those soldiers who died but never left Winchester.

One of the more popular stories that is told on ghost tours is that of the Patton brothers. Their epitaph includes lines from *Paradise and the Peri*, by Thomas Moore. It reads:

> *Here lie asleep in one grave The Patton Brothers*
> *Oh, if there be on this earthly sphere*
> *A boon, an offering heaven holds dear,*
> *'Tis the last libation Liberty draws*
> *From the heart that bleeds and breaks in her cause!*
> *George S. and W. Tazewell Patton are buried*

The Patton brothers, General George S. Patton, who was mortally wounded during the Third Battle of Winchester, and W. Tazewell, who died at Gettysburg, are said to have a visitor come to their grave somewhat frequently. Reports say that a man who is small in stature and wearing a military coat and hat visits the grave and tilts his head in reverence to the brothers.[310] Visiting a grave is not so frightening. It is when witnesses have approached the man and he disappears that the scene becomes eerie. General George S. Patton was the grandfather of the general of World War II who holds the same name.[311] Exactly who this man is and why he visits the grave are left to speculation.

Another ghostly story involves Stonewall Cemetery of Mount Hebron and the National Cemetery that is directly across the street. This is one of my favorite Virginia ghost stories, especially knowing that the Civil War was a complicated conflict that had brothers fighting brothers. As the story is told, while the sun begins to set, those who are driving or even walking by the cemeteries can see ghostly gray forms rising from the Confederate cemetery. These raggedy forms make their way across the street to the National Cemetery. The beauty of the story is that when the ghostly forms from the National Cemetery rise up to meet the ghostly forms from the Confederate cemetery, there is no fighting. There is no more sickness or battles. The war is over, and all of the soldiers can finally rest. They have returned to being American brothers once again.[312]

THE OMINOUS END

As we conclude the tour of the haunted cemeteries in Shenandoah Valley, images of Civil War apparitions and lore about statues stay with me. I am glad to have learned about Eva Clark and her legacy, and I am saddened to learn about the grief of Martha Jordan that led to her premature burial. May each of these individuals truly be at rest.

CONCLUSION

Historic cemeteries are among America's most vital cultural resources, serving as keepers of our collective past. Each cemetery has a multitude of stories that offer glimpses into the lives and struggles of those in the communities that came before us. These burial grounds are more than final resting places; they are open-air archives that offer a way to preserve people's legacies.

Ghostlore remains important today, because it connects us to the past in ways that are both emotional and cultural, and it transcends generations. In a time when we rely heavily on technology, ghost stories remind us of life's mysteries; they spark curiosity and imagination. We do not necessarily pick up local newspapers like we once did. We access our news from various media outlets. Ghostlore helps preserve local history and traditions, and it can spotlight forgotten people, places and events that might otherwise fade into obscurity. The world may feel as if it is rapidly changing, but these spooky tales bridge the gap between past and present while they encourage us to explore deeper meanings behind the unexplained. Throughout my journey of Virginia's cemeteries, the ghost stories shared explore themes of mortality, memory and the unknown. I learned about folk art tombstones, visited a cemetery that was established after a mining disaster and overcame my own slithering fears when hiking the Appalachian Trail. I slept in haunted inns, discovered fascinating facts about past presidents and national heroes. I visited a grave that had been struck by lightning multiple times, encountered strange weather phenomena, met a man named Ghost, learned about a cemetery's "resident ghost" and watched for apparitions of those who were mortally wounded during the Civil War.

The ghostlore that surrounds Virginia cemeteries often reveals deeper truths about history, memory and identity and gives voice to the forgotten stories. By exploring the cemetery grounds, the historic records and the folklore that lingers, we honor those buried there and exhume valuable insights into our shared heritage. These spaces remind us that the past is always present and is just waiting to be remembered.

I have always liked stories and storytellers. Old newspaper articles include some of the best tales of the past. I like to design cemetery tours around themes. I love the research involved, and I love visiting cemeteries and meeting the people who are included in my books.

There are so many buried stories that need to be discovered. I hope that along your cemetery travels, you find an amazing story. I hope we can all confront our own ghosts and find peace. Until we run into each other in one of Virginia's cemeteries, you might consider attending one of the many spooky or historic cemetery tours and events in your region.

GHOSTLY FOCUSED CEMETERY TOURS

CENTRAL VIRGINIA

Fancy Me Mad, Historic St. John's Church, October, https://www.historicstjohnschurch.org/events

A Witches Walk through Hollywood Cemetery, River City Witches, October, https://www.facebook.com/RiverCityWitches

All Hallows Eve at Blandford Church Cemetery, City of Petersburg's Museums, October, http://www.petersburgva.gov/

Historic Tuckahoe Self-Guided Tour, year-round, https://www.visithistorictuckahoe.com/self-guided-tour/

Maplewood Cemetery, US Ghost Adventures, year-round, https://usghostadventures.com/charlottesville-ghost-tour/maplewood-cemetery/

NORTHERN VIRGINIA

Haunted Historic House & Cemetery Tour, Historic Dumfries Virginia, October, https://historicdumfriesva.org/purchase-tickets/

Ghost & Graveyard Tours, Alexandria Colonial Tours, seasonal, https://www.alexcolonialtours.com/
Ghosts of Fredericksburg, Virginia: A Self-Guided Walking Tour Including St. George's Graveyard, year-round, https://actiontourguide.com
Haunted History Tour, Middleburg Ghost Tours, seasonal, https://middleburgghosttours.com

Tidewater and Coastal Virginia

Cemetery Tours, Colonial Ghosts, year-round, https://theghosttour.com/
Legends of Main Street: A Suffolk Ghost Walk, Suffolk Tourism, seasonal, https://www.visitsuffolkva.com/events/
Letting the Dead Rest in Peace (A Halloween Cemetery Picnic), Cedar Hill Cemetery, October, https://nsccva.org/tours/
Twilight Cemetery Tours, St. Luke's Historic Museum & Church, October, https://stlukesmuseum.org/calendar/

Blue Ridge and Southwest Virginia

Candlelight Tours at Old City Cemetery, Lynchburg, October, https://www.gravegarden.org/
The Ghosts of Historic Lynchburg, Presbyterian Cemetery on Grace Street, October, https://www.lynchburghistoricalfoundation.org/
East Hill Cemetery Ghost Walk, Sullivan County Department of Archives and Tourism, year-round, https://www.bristolhistoricalassociation.com

Shenandoah Valley

Staunton's Ghost Tours, US Ghost Adventures, year-round, https://usghostadventures.com/staunton-ghost-tour/
Strasburg Heritage Association Bi-Annual Ghost Tours, October, https://www.strasburgva.com/
Guided Walking Tour of Old Town Winchester History, The Winchester-Frederick County Convention & Visitors Bureau, May–October, https://visitwinchesterva.com/guided-tours/

NOTES

INTRODUCTION

1. Quote credited to Reverend Dr. W.A.R. Goodwin, shared in Ivor Noël Hume, "Doctor Goodwin's Ghosts: A Tale of Midnight and Wythe House Mysteries," *Colonial Williamsburg Journal* (Spring 2001). https://research.colonialwilliamsburg.org/foundation/journal/Spring01/wythe_ghosts.cfm.
2. "Ghostly Haunts," Virginia Is for Lovers, https://www.virginia.org/things-to-do/tours/ghosts-and-haunted-tours/.
3. Edrick Thay, *Haunted Cemeteries: True Tales from Beyond the Grave* (Ghost House Books, 2004), 9; Hume, "Doctor Goodwin's Ghosts."
4. Hume, "Doctor Goodwin's Ghosts."
5. Alena R. Pirok, "The Common Uncanny: Ghostlore and the Creation of Virginia History" (PhD diss., University of South Florida, 2017), 161, https://digitalcommons.usf.edu/etd/6929.
6. Hume, "Doctor Goodwin's Ghosts."
7. Pirok, "Common Uncanny," 161.
8. *Alexandria* (VA) *Gazette*, June 15, 1870, 2.
9. *Virginian-Pilot*, December 21, 1902, 2.

CHAPTER 1

10. "Hollywood Cemetery," The Cultural Landscape Foundation, https://tclf.org/landscapes/hollywood-cemetery.
11. Stephan J. Kunitz, "Mortality Change in America, 1620–1920," *Human Biology* 56, no. 3 (1984): 559–82.

12. "Snake-Handlers Live Up to Name," *Richmond Times-Dispatch*, October 31, 1985, 51.
13. Misty Thomas, "A Ghostly Woody and a Dead Little Girl," *Quail Bell Magazine*, September 5, 2013, http://www.quailbellmagazine.com/the-real/living-folklore-the-ghost-dog-of-hollywood-cemetery.
14. *Richmond* (VA) *Dispatch*, February 8, 1862, 3.
15. James E. DuPriest Jr., *Hollywood Cemetery: A Tour* (A Richmond Discoveries Publication, 1989), 13.
16. "New Collections: Sailor the Iron Dog," Baltimore Museum of Industry, https://www.thebmi.org/portfolio/sailor-the-iron-dog/.
17. Nicole Kappatos, "Richmond Dog Lived like an Heiress after Her Famous Owner Passed Away in 1945," *Richmond Times-Dispatch*, February 26, 2019, https://richmond.com/from-the-archives/richmond-dog-lived-like-an-heiress-after-her-famous-owner-passed-away-in-1945/article_6b86de67-05bd-5bfc-a626-ec065ebc4b47.html.
18. Tricia Pearsall, "Ellen Glasgow's Richmond," in *Regarding Ellen Glasgow: Essays for Contemporary Readers* (The Library of Virginia, 2001), 192.
19. "W.W. Pool: The Richmond Vampire?" *The Dead Bell*, October 28, 2015, https://thedeadbelldotcom1.wordpress.com/2015/10/28/w-w-pool-the-richmond-vampire/; "Hold Mosby Funeral," *Richmond* (VA) *Times Dispatch*, October 4, 1925.
20. Garry F. Curtis, "Time Flies in 'Perfect Jewel,'" *The Commonwealth Times* 7, no. 25 (April 30, 1976): 12–13.
21. Curtis, "Time Flies," 12.
22. Em Holter, "Whispers from the Grave: Richmond's 19th-Century Struggle with Grave Robbery," *Richmond* (VA) *Times Dispatch*, November 18, 2023.
23. Curtis, "Time Flies," 12.
24. Harry Kollatz Jr., "No Interview with a Vampire," *Richmond Magazine*, October 1993, 11.
25. Scott Bergman and Sandi Bergman, *Haunted Richmond: The Shadows of Shockoe* (The History Press, 2007), 64.
26. Kollatz Jr., "No Interview," 11.
27. *Richmond* (VA) *Dispatch*, December 19, 1866, 2.
28. *Richmond* (VA) *Dispatch*, May 16, 1876, 1.
29. *Richmond* (VA) *Dispatch*, August 16, 1883, 1.
30. *Richmond* (VA) *Dispatch*, June 15, 1897, 6.
31. *The Times Dispatch* (Richmond, VA), February 27, 1922, 7.
32. Certificate of Death, Commonwealth of Virginia, 3,465–490. The certificate lists his age of death as seventy-nine. Being born in 1841 and passing in 1922 would have made Pool eighty-one at the time of his death.

33. *The Times Dispatch* (Richmond, VA), March 1, 1922, 3.
34. "Samuel R. Owens Dies at Floyd Avenue Home," *The Times Dispatch* (Richmond, VA), February 27, 1922, 7.
35. David K. Nartonis, "The Rise of 19th-Century American Spiritualism, 1854–1873," *Journal for the Scientific Study of Religion* (2010): 361.
36. Pamela E. Apkarian-Russell, *Washington's Haunted Past: Capital Ghosts of America* (The History Press, 2006), 45.
37. George L. Christian, *The Capitol Disaster: A Chapter of Reconstruction in Virginia* (Richmond Press Inc., 1915), 1.
38. *Alexandria* (VA) *Gazette*, June 15, 1870, 2.
39. *Memphis* (TN) *Daily Appeal*, June 26, 1870, 1.
40. *The Baltimore* (MD) *Sun*, June 15, 1870, 4.
41. *Memphis* (TN) *Daily Appeal*, June 26, 1870, 1.
42. *Richmond* (VA) *Dispatch*, August 19, 1870, 1.
43. Jeff Bahr, Troy Taylor and Loren Coleman, "Crying for the Colonel," in *Weird Virginia* (Sterling Publishing Co., 2007), 240.
44. The two other cemeteries that hold the remains of two U.S. presidents are Arlington National Cemetery, where John F. Kennedy and William Howard Taft are buried, and United First Parish in Quincy, Massachusetts, where John Adams and John Quincy Adams are buried.
45. "Nomination Form: James Monroe Tomb," National Register of Historic Places Inventory, July 1969, 271, https://npgallery.nps.gov/NRHP/GetAsset/NHLS/71001044_text.
46. "Dead Presidents Still Haunting Their Homes in Virginia?" *Amy's Crypt*, March 7, 2018, https://amyscrypt.com/dead-presidents-virginia/.
47. Evan Andrews, "7 Presidential War Stories," History Channel, September 2, 2014, https://www.history.com/news/7-presidential-war-stories.

CHAPTER 2

48. "The Year 1811," *Pittsburgh Gazette*, April 10, 1812, 3, http://history.hanover.edu/texts/1811.
49. Misty Thomas, "A Graveyard Beneath the Sanctuary," *Quail Bell Magazine*, September 5, 2013, http://www.quailbellmagazine.com/the-real/archives/09-2013/3.
50. "A Holiday Horror Story: The Richmond Theatre Fire of 1811," Norfolk Towne Assembly, December 21, 2020, https://www.facebook.com/photo/?fbid=1107001986439127&set=a.362234830915850.

Chapter 3

51. "FAQ," Historic St. Johns Church, https://www.historicstjohnschurch.org.
52. "Welcome to Richmond Ghosts," US Ghost Adventures, https://usghostadventures.com/richmond-ghost-tour/.
53. "Welcome," US Ghost Adventures.
54. "Patrick Henry's Scotchtown," Facebook posts, June 23, 2016, and September 4, 2016.
55. Beth Copenhaver, "This Hospital in Virginia Has a Dark and Evil History That Will Never Be Forgotten." OnlyInYourState, June 23, 2016, https://www.onlyinyourstate.com/state-pride/virginia/abandoned-hospital-in-virginia.
56. Rose Gallenberger, "Patrick and Sarah Henry: Mental Illness in 18th-Century America," National Museum of American History, July 2, 2015, https://americanhistory.si.edu/explore/stories/patrick-and-sarah-henry-mental-illness-18th-century-america.
57. Gallenberger, "Patrick and Sarah Henry."
58. Catherine Armstrong, "The Most Terrifying Ghost Story to Ever Come Out of Virginia Is Truly Chilling," OnlyInYourState, October 18, 2016, https://www.onlyinyourstate.com/virginia/scotchtown-ghost-story-va/.
59. "Sarah Henry: Patrick Henry's Basement Kept Wife," Richmond Ghost Tours, https://rvaghosts.com/sarah-henry-patrick-henrys-basement-kept-wife/.
60. "Welcome," US Ghost Adventures.
61. "Welcome," US Ghost Adventures.
62. Jon Kukla, *Patrick Henry: Champion of Liberty* (Simon & Schuster, 2017), 158–60.

Chapter 4

63. "Franklin Street Burying Ground," Congregation Beth Ahabah, https://www.bethahabah.org/bama/hebrew-cemetery/; Claire Millhiser Rosenbaum, "By-Laws, Rules and Regulations of the Hebrew Cemetery Company of Richmond," Congregation Beth Ahabah, October 31, 2012, 3.
64. Rosenbaum, "By-Laws, Rules and Regulations," 5.
65. Rosenbaum, "By-Laws, Rules and Regulations," 4.
66. Rosenbaum, "By-Laws, Rules and Regulations," 4.
67. Rosenbaum, "By-Laws, Rules and Regulations," 5.
68. "Franklin Street Burying Ground," Congregation Beth Ahabah.

Chapter 5

69. "National Cemetery Administration," U.S. Department of Veterans Affairs, www.cem.va.gov.

70. "Cold Harbor," American Battlefield Trust, https://www.battlefields.org/learn/civil-war/battles/cold-harbor.
71. "The Spirit of Cold Harbor," *Your Ghost Stories*, February 26, 2020, https://www.yourghoststories.com/real-ghost-story.php?story=27136.
72. "Spirit of Cold Harbor," *Your Ghost Stories*.
73. "Haunted Tales: The Cold Harbor Battlefield," *The Purcell Chronicles*, June 13, 2018, https://thepurcellchronicles.blogspot.com/2018/06/haunted-tales-cold-harbor-battlefield.html.
74. "National Cemetery Administration," U.S. Department of Veterans Affairs.
75. I told you that you would meet a Ghost!
76. Virginia law prohibits entering a cemetery at nighttime without the consent of the owner, proprietor or custodian for any purpose other than to visit the burial lot or grave of some family member. Trespassers will be found guilty of a class 4 misdemeanor.
77. Department of Veterans Affairs, "National Cemetery Administration (NCA) Facilities Design Guide," June 2000, section 5 revised March 10, 2010.

CHAPTER 6

78. Robert Van Ness, "Special Halloween Episode: Haunted Tuckahoe," *Virginia History Podcast*, October 28, 2020, https://vahistorypodcast.com/2020/10/28/special-halloween-episode-haunted-tuckahoe/. This podcast includes an interview with Jessica Stith, researcher and tour guide.
79. "Gray Ladies," Occult World, https://occult-world.com/gray-ladies/.
80. Van Ness, "Haunted Tuckahoe."
81. Alan Pell Crawford, "In the Midnight Hour: Tales of the Gray Lady and Other Great Virginia Ghosts," *Virginia Living*, September 10, 2015, 46.
82. Martha Steger, "A Ghost Story at Tuckahoe Plantation," *Richmond* (VA) *Times Dispatch*, August 5, 2020, https://richmond.com/news/local/goochland/article_cb2a6ed1-20c1-5de0-a68f-8f5f729e968a.html.
83. Steger, "Ghost Story."
84. Harlane Lane, *When the Mind Hears: A History of the Deaf* (Vintage Press, 1984), 156.
85. Francis Biddle, "Scandal at Bizarre," *American Heritage* 12, no. 5 (August 1961), https://www.americanheritage.com/scandal-bizarre.
86. Lane, *When the Mind Hears*, 156.
87. Van Ness, "Haunted Tuckahoe." The word *haint* is an alternative spelling of *haunt*.
88. Rosemary Ellen Guiley, *The Encyclopedia of Ghosts and Spirits* (Checkmark Books, 2007), 204; "Gray Ladies," Occult World.
89. Guiley, *Encyclopedia of Ghosts and Spirits*, 204.

Chapter 7

90. "Blandford Cemetery," Petersburg, https://www.petersburgva.gov/303/Blandford-Cemetery.
91. "Major General William Phillips," Petersburg, http://www.petersburg-va.org/484/Major-General-William-Phillips.
92. "Blandford Cemetery," Petersburg.
93. "Blandford Cemetery," Historic Petersburg Foundation, http://www.historicpetersburg.org/blandford-cemetery/.
94. "Blandford Cemetery," Petersburg.
95. "The Blandford Cemetery in Petersburg Is One of Virginia's Spookiest Cemeteries," Only in Your State, August 28, 2019, https://www.onlyinyourstate.com/virginia/blandford-cemetery-haunted-va/.
96. Mary Cherry Allen, "Local Garden Club Undertakes Improvement of Cemetery Here," *The Progress-Index*, February 5, 1961, 13.
97. Allen, "Local Garden Club," 13.
98. Katherine Calos, "Blandford Is More Than Resting Place," *Richmond Times-Dispatch*, October 25, 1998, J1.
99. Quote shared in L.B. Taylor Jr., *Haunted Virginia* (Stackpole Books, 2009), 54–55.
100. "Sarcophagus or Metallic Burial Cases," advertisement in *Richmond Daily Times*, March 22, 1851, 3.

Chapter 9

101. "Maplewood Cemetery," Charlottesville Ghost Tours, https://usghostadventures.com/charlottesville-ghost-tour/maplewood-cemetery/.
102. "Maplewood Cemetery," CVillePedia, https://www.cvillepedia.org/Maplewood_Cemetery.
103. "Maplewood Cemetery," Charlottesville Ghost Tours.
104. "Maplewood Cemetery," Charlottesville Ghost Tours.
105. "Fantastic Antics of Moon Ghost Enliven Albemarle Society Meet," *The Farmville* (VA) *Herald*, August 16, 1940, 7.
106. Anna Mary Moon, *Sketches of the Moon and Barclay Families, Including the Harris, Moorman, Johnson, Appling Families*, compiled by Anna Mary Moon (n.p., 1939), 11.
107. "Fantastic Antics of Moon Ghost Enliven Albemarle Society Meet," *The Farmville* (VA) *Herald*, August 16, 1940, 7.
108. "Fantastic Antics," *The Farmville* (VA) *Herald*, 7.
109. "Fantastic Antics," *The Farmville* (VA) *Herald*, 7.
110. "Fantastic Antics," *The Farmville* (VA) *Herald*, 7.
111. Moon, *Sketches of the Moon and Barclay Families*, 13.

112. Rick Britton, "Local Haunt: The Moon Ghost of Albemarle," *C-VILLE Weekly* (Charlottesville, VA), October 28, 2015, https://www.c-ville.com/local-haunt-moon-ghost-albemarle/.
113. "Fantastic Antics," *The Farmville* (VA) *Herald*, 7.
114. "Fantastic Antics," *The Farmville* (VA) *Herald*, 7.
115. "Fantastic Antics," *The Farmville* (VA) *Herald*, 7.
116. Moon, *Sketches of the Moon and Barclay Families*, 16.

Chapter 10

117. David A. Maurer, "Set in Stone: The Serenity of UVA's Cemetery Belies a Colorful Past," *The University of Virginia Magazine* (Spring 2008), https://uvamagazine.org/articles/set_in_stone; *Richmond Enquirer*, April 21, 1846, 4.
118. *Richmond Enquirer*, May 26, 1846, 4.
119. Sarah Lindenfeld Hall, "School Spirits: Tales of Things That Have Gone Bump—Or Step-Thump—on Grounds," *The University of Virginia Magazine* 113, no. 3 (Fall 2024): 30–37.
120. David A. Maurer, "Robbing Graves to Learn," *The Daily Progress* (Charlottesville, VA), August 10, 2008, C1.
121. Maurer, "Robbing Graves."

Chapter 11

122. "Thomas Jefferson's Original Tombstone, University of Missouri, Columbia, Missouri," Atlas Obscura, May 8, 2018, https://www.atlasobscura.com/places/thomas-jeffersons-original-tombstone.
123. "Jefferson's Gravesite," Monticello, https://www.monticello.org/visit/tips-for-visiting/jefferson-s-gravesite/.
124. "The Thomas Jefferson Center for Historic Plants," Monticello, https://www.monticello.org/house-gardens/center-for-historic-plants/.
125. "The Thomas Jefferson Center for Historic Plants," Monticello.
126. Tiya Miles, "How Ghost Tours Often Exploit African-American History," *Here & Now*, WBUR, NPR, October 30, 2015, https://www.wbur.org/hereandnow/2015/10/30/ghost-tours-african-american-history.
127. "The Life of Sally Hemings," Monticello, https://www.monticello.org/sallyhemings/.
128. Lucian K. Truscott IV, "Children of Monticello," *American Heritage* 52, no. 1 (February/March 2001), https://www.americanheritage.com/children-monticello#.
129. Colin Dickey, "The Hidden Ghosts of America's Slave Past," *The New York Times*, October 30, 2023, https://www.nytimes.com/2023/10/30/opinion/ghosts-america-slavery-past.html.

130. L.B. Taylor Jr., "The Mystery Hummer of Monticello," *The Ghosts of Charlottesville and Lynchburg…And Nearby Environs* (Progress Printing Co., 1992), 30.
131. Taylor Jr., "Mystery Hummer of Monticello," 30.
132. "Jefferson's Gravestone," Monticello, https://www.monticello.org/research-education/thomas-jefferson-encyclopedia/jeffersons-gravestone/.
133. "Coins on Jefferson's Grave," Monticello, https://www.monticello.org/research-education/thomas-jefferson-encyclopedia/coins-jeffersons-grave/.
134. "The Monticello Graveyard" signage at the grave of Thomas Jefferson.
135. Shawn Donley and Marianne Donley, "The Haunting of Jefferson's Monticello—Our Haunted Travels," PANICd, May 15, 2018, https://www.youtube.com/@OurHauntedTravels.

CHAPTER 12

136. "Dead Presidents?" *Amy's Crypt.*
137. "Payne Todd, the Wrathful Ghost of Montpelier Plantations," *The Daily Progress* (Charlottesville, VA), October 25, 2006, 26.
138. Taylor Jr., *Ghosts of Charlottesville and Lynchburg*, 146–48.
139. C. Thomas Chapman, "Who Was Buried in James Madison's Grave?" (master of arts thesis, William & Mary, 2005), 236.
140. Minutes, Hollywood Cemetery Company, records 1847–1929, section one, minute book, June 23, 1847–March 26, 1868 (Mss3 H7298a1), Virginia Historical Society.
141. *Fredericksburg* (VA) *News*, October 6, 1857.
142. "Dead Presidents?" *Amy's Crypt.*
143. Libby McNamee, "The Ghost of Dolley Madison," https://libbymcnamee.com/the-ghost-of-dolley-madison-2/.
144. Walt Harrington, "Ghosts of Montpelier," HistoryNet, https://www.historynet.com/ghosts-of-montpelier/
145. Chapman, "Who Was Buried," 20.
146. Elizabeth Dowling Taylor, *A Slave in the White House: Paul Jennings and the Madisons* (Palgrave Macmillan, 2012), 224.

CHAPTER 13

147. Reverend W.M. Clark, *St. George's Cemetery: An Historical Sketch* (Ladies Cemetery Guild, 1892), 4.
148. Clark, *St. George's Cemetery*, 5.
149. Marguerite DuPont Lee, *Virginia Ghosts*, rev. ed. (Virginia Book Company, 1966), 21.
150. Clark, *George's Cemetery*, 5.
151. "Tours," St. George's Graveyard, https://stgraves.churchsp.org.

Chapter 14

152. Joanna Wilson Green, "Remembering What We'd Rather Forget—*Memento Mori*," The Virginia Department of Historic Resources, July 15, 2021, https://www.dhr.virginia.gov/blog-posts/remembering-what-wed-rather-forget-memento-mori/.
153. DuPont Lee, *Virginia Ghosts*, 25.
154. DuPont Lee, *Virginia Ghosts*, 26.

Chapter 15

155. Henry Wiencek, "George Washington (1732–1799)," *Encyclopedia Virginia*, December 7, 2020.
156. Emily Dickinson to Elizabeth Holland (L179), March 18, 1855, in *The Letters of Emily Dickinson*, ed. Thomas H. Johnson (Belknap Press of Harvard University Press, 1958), 2:318–19.
157. Jessie MacLeod, "William Lee (fl. 1768–1810)," *Encyclopedia Virginia*, December 7, 2020, https://encyclopediavirginia.org/entries/lee-william-fl-1768-1810.
158. Jan Mackell Collins, "The Twisted History of Washington's Mount Vernon," Grunge, January 23, 2023, https://www.grunge.com/242012/the-twisted-history-of-washingtons-mount-vernon/.
159. MacLeod, "William Lee," *Encyclopedia Virginia*.
160. "George Washington's Ghost," *The Galion* (OH) *Inquirer*, April 14, 1881, 2.
161. "Spooky Wails Haunt Mount Vernon," *The Daily Progress* (Charlottesville, VA), May 18, 1979, 15.

Chapter 16

162. "Ghost Captured," *Alexandria Gazette*, Mar 4, 1895.
163. "Ghost Captured," *Alexandria Gazette*.
164. For more information, read *Sin in the Second City: Madams, Ministers, Playboys, and the Battle for America's Soul* (Random House, 2008) by Karen Abbott, which goes into more details about the lives of the sisters.

Chapter 18

165. "Rediscover Haunted Arlington," Arlington Public Library, October 28, 2019, https://library.arlingtonva.us/2019/10/28/rediscover-haunted-arlington/.
166. Airborne08, "Tales from the U.S. Army Old Guard and Tomb Guards," posted in 2014 on r/nosleep, Reddit, https://www.reddit.com/r/nosleep/comments/3jj1p1/tales_from_the_us_army_old_guard_and_tomb_guards.

167. Airborne08, "Tales."
168. Leslie Lieber, "The Legend of Ghosts in the White House: Presidential Spooks," *The Virginian-Pilot* (Norfolk, VA), April 25, 1954, 29.
169. Archibald Butt to Clara Butt, July 26, 1911, in *Taft and Roosevelt: The Intimate Letters of Archie Butt, Military Aide*, vol. 2 (Doubleday, Doran and Co., 1930), 715–18.
170. "White House Is Notorious Haunt of Ghosts; Nobody Ever Minded Living There, However," *Washington* (D.C.) *Herald*, March 2, 1913, 3.
171. Lieber, "Legend of Ghosts in the White House," 28–29.
172. "President William Howard Taft Memorial Grave," Arlington National Cemetery, https://www.arlingtoncemetery.mil/Explore/Monuments-and-Memorials/President-William-H-Taft-Gravesite.
173. Lyndon B. Johnson, *Public Papers of the Presidents of the United States*, vol. 1 (Government Printing Office, 1965), 1–10, 218.
174. "History," Union Oyster House, http://unionoysterhouse.com/pages/history.html.
175. Nico Danilovich, "JFK's Ghost Allegedly Hangs Out in a Boston Seafood Joint," Tasting Table, October 17, 2022, https://www.tastingtable.com/1056752/jfks-ghost-allegedly-hangs-out-in-a-boston-seafood-joint/.
176. "President John Fitzgerald Kennedy Gravesite," Arlington National Cemetery, https://www.arlingtoncemetery.mil/Explore/Monuments-and-Memorials/President-John-F-Kennedy-Gravesite.
177. Christopher Coleman, "The Haunted Homes of the Robert E. Lee," *Dixie Spirits Blog*, November 2, 2018, https://ckc4me.wordpress.com/2018/11/02/the-haunted-homes-of-the-robert-e-lee/.

Chapter 20

178. Kerry Phelps Dale, "Middleburg Ghost Tours," *Middleburg Life*, October 2018, https://www.middleburglife.com/middleburg-ghost-tours/.

Chapter 21

179. L.B. Taylor Jr., "The Triple Ghosts of Westover," in *The Ghosts of Williamsburg…And Nearby Environs* (Progress Printing Co., 1983), 78.
180. Taylor Jr., "Triple Ghosts of Westover," 78.
181. "Evelyn Byrd," Historic Westover, https://historicwestover.com/evelyn-byrd.htm.

Chapter 22

182. "As Times Changed…," Westover Episcopal Church, https://westoverepiscopalchurch.org/history/.

183. DuPont Lee, *Virginia Ghosts*, 107.
184. "Edgewood Plantation Bed and Breakfast," Virginia Is for Lovers, https://www.virginia.org/listing/edgewood-plantation-bed-and-breakfast/10990/.
185. Julian Boulware, personal discussion at Edgewood, May 17, 2023.
186. Alena R. Pirok, *The Common Uncanny: Ghostlore and the Creation of Virginia History* (University of South Florida, 2017), 62.
187. DuPont Lee, *Virginia Ghosts*, 108.
188. Taylor Jr., "Lost Love at Edgewood," in *The Ghosts of Williamsburg*, 54.
189. DuPont Lee, *Virginia Ghosts*, 108.

Chapter 23

190. Taylor Jr., "The Gray Lady of Sherwood Forest," in *The Ghosts of Williamsburg*, 36.
191. Taylor Jr., "Gray Lady of Sherwood Forest," 38.

Chapter 24

192. "Old Haunts," W&M Style, William & Mary, https://www.wm.edu/style/old-haunts.php.
193. "21 Burial Sites and Possible 18th-Century Building Found at Colonial Williamsburg Site," WAVY (Williamsburg, VA), July 15, 2021, https://www.wavy.com/news/local-news/williamsburg/21-burial-sites-and-possible-18th-century-building-found-at-colonial-williamsburg-site/; "The Forgotten Graves of Williamsburg," *Colonial Ghosts*, August 15, 2017, https://colonialghosts.com/the-forgotten-graves-of-williamsburg/.
194. "Why Is Williamsburg Haunted?" Colonial Ghosts, August 15, 2017, https://colonialghosts.com/why-is-williamsburg-haunted/; "Civil War (April 12, 1861–May 9, 1865," Special Collections Research Center Knowledgebase, William & Mary Libraries, https://scrc-kb.libraries.wm.edu/civil-war-april-12-1861-may-9-1865.
195. Hannah Strouth, "Behind the Brick Walls: Wren Crypt Holds a History Beneath Your Feet," *The Flat Hat*, November 2, 2015, https://flathatnews.com/2015/11/02/behind-the-brick-walls-wren-crypt-holds-a-history-beneath-your-feet/.
196. Strouth, "Behind the Brick Walls."
197. "College Cemetery," Special Collections Research Center Knowledgebase, William & Mary Libraries, https://scrc-kb.libraries.wm.edu/college-cemetery.

Chapter 25

198. "Bruton Parish Churchyard: A Self-Guided Tour," Bruton Parish Church, https://www.brutonparish.org/history.
199. Robert Doares, "The Life and Literature of Nathaniel Beverley Tucker," *Colonial Williamsburg Journal* (Autumn 2001). https://research.colonialwilliamsburg.org/Foundation/journal/Autumn01/tucker.cfm.
200. Poe's review of George Balcombe, *Southern Literary Messenger* 3, no. 1 (January 1837): 49–58.
201. Molly Feser, "Oddities & Curiosities: Nathaniel Beverley Tucker's Tombstone," *Williamsburg Yorktown Daily*, October 29, 2021, https://wydaily.com/latest-news/2021/10/29/oddities-curiosities-nathaniel-beverley-tuckers-tombstone/.
202. "Nathaniel Beverley Tucker (1820–1890)," Special Collections Research Knowledgebase, William & Mary Libraries, https://scrc-kb.libraries.wm.edu/nathaniel-beverley-tucker-1820-1890.
203. "Disturbing the Dead," *The Daily Press* (Newport News, VA), November 10, 1938, 4.
204. "Churchyard Closes," *The Virginia Gazette* (Williamsburg, VA), March 28, 1998, 5.
205. Jackie Eileen Behrend, "Long-Ago Lovers Unite in the George Wythe House," in *The Hauntings of Williamsburg, Yorktown, and Jamestown* (John F. Blair, 2006), 48.
206. DuPont Lee, *Virginia Ghosts*, 92.
207. DuPont Lee, *Virginia Ghosts*, 92.
208. DuPont Lee, *Virginia Ghosts*, 92–93.
209. L.B. Taylor Jr., "The Legend of Lady Skipwith," in *The Ghosts of Williamsburg*, 33–34.
210. Taylor Jr., "Legend of Lady Skipwith," 35.
211. Behrend, "Long-Ago Lovers," 48.
212. "Romance Revealed by Graves in Old Bruton Churchyard," *The Virginia Gazette* (Williamsburg, VA), September 23, 1938, 5.
213. "Free Inhabitants in the City of Williamsburg in the County of James City," 1850 United States Federal Census, October 3, 1850.
214. "Bruton Parish Church," Williamsburg Ghost Tour, https://williamsburgghosttour.com/bruton-parish-church/.
215. "Bruton Parish Church," Williamsburg Ghost Tour.
216. "Bruton Parish Church," Williamsburg Ghost Tour.
217. "Bruton Parish Church," Williamsburg Ghost Tour.

Chapter 26

218. Caitlin Verboon, Dr. Thomas H. Taylor, "Historic Area Graveyard Study, Colonial Williamsburg Foundation Library Research Report Series–0383," Colonial Williamsburg Foundation Library, 2005, https://research.colonialwilliamsburg.org/DigitalLibrary/.
219. *Virginia Gazette* (Williamsburg, VA), July 7, 1906, 8.

Chapter 27

220. "History," St. Luke's Historic Church & Museum, https://stlukesmuseum.org/history/.
221. "Cemeteries," St. Luke's Historic Church & Museum, https://stlukesmuseum.org/cemetery/.
222. Katherine Hill, "Video Enhancing Visits to St. Luke's," *The Smithfield Times*, August 10, 1994, 7.
223. Hill, "Video Enhancing Visits."
224. L.B. Taylor Jr., "What's Good for the Goose," in *The Ghosts of Virginia*, vol. 4 (Progress Printing Co., 1998), 94395.
225. M. Silva, "Historic Cemetery Series: St. Luke's Graveyard (Smithfield, VA)," *A Collection of Interesting Local History*, June 25, 2016, https://elephantsmarch.wordpress.com/2016/06/25/st-lukes-graveyard-smithfield-va/; Our Strange Reality, "Haunted Virginia: St. Luke's Church, Phantoms in the Graveyard," April 18, 2021, https://youtu.be/f0zxGf9kpPs?si=4MuZgmpnpVoctuQH.
226. Hill, "Video Enhancing Visits."
227. "Upcoming Events," St. Luke's Historic Church & Museum, https://stlukesmuseum.org/calendar/

Chapter 28

228. "Cemeteries," Suffolk, Virginia, https://www.suffolkva.us/1516/Cemeteries.
229. Ashley McDougal, "Cedar Hill Cemetery Ghosts of Suffolk Episode 2," Sell757, https://youtu.be/f1CpF_RU_qA?si=xtdH1j7KIHBAPDmj.
230. McDougal, "Cedar Hill Cemetery Ghosts."
231. *Cedar Hill Cemetery: Suffolk, Virginia* (Visit Suffolk, 2020), 1–16, https://issuu.com/suffolktourism/docs/cedarhillcemetery.
232. Visit Suffolk, Virginia, https://www.visitsuffolkva.com/.

Chapter 29

233. Amy Waters Yarsinske, *Norfolk's Church Street: Between Memory and Reality* (Arcadia Publishing, 1999), 20.
234. "Haunted Norfolk," Mid-Atlantic Tourism Public Relations Alliance, October 18, 2020, https://matpra.org/haunted-norfolk-va/.
235. Kelly Sowell, "Snowden Angel and Artist William Couper," Elmwood Cemetery, https://www.elmwoodcemetery.org/blog/posts/snowden-angel-and-artist-william-couper.
236. "William Couper," Elmwood Cemetery, https://www.historicforrest.com/HSites/NorfolkVA/elmwoodCemetery/williamCouper.html.
237. "Was It a Ghost, or Did He See 'Em?" *Virginia-Pilot* (Norfolk, VA), December 21, 1902, 2.

Chapter 30

238. Old City Cemetery, https://www.gravegarden.org/.

Chapter 31

239. "Notables," Spring Hill Cemetery, http://www.springhillcemetery.org/notables/
240. "Deaths in Virginia," *The Baltimore* (MD) *Sun*, June 24, 1910, 12.
241. "Miss Cornelia Clopton," *The Times Dispatch* (Richmond, VA), March 29, 1917, 3; State of Montana Certificate of Death, March 26, 1917.
242. "A Special Story for Halloween," *The Bee* (Danville, VA), October 31, 1977, 11-B.
243. Illustration in *Harper's Weekly*, October 26, 1861, 688.
244. Josephine Pollard, "Girls on Halloween," *The Richmond Dispatch*, November 1, 1896, 6.

Chapter 32

245. Ann Marshall Whitley, *Ghost Stories and Mysteries of Sweet Briar* (Alumnae Association of Sweet Briar College, 1992), i.
246. Daniel W. Barefoot, *Haunted Halls of Ivy: Ghosts of Southern Colleges and Universities* (John F. Blair, 2004), 174.
247. Barefoot, *Haunted Halls of Ivy*, 174.
248. Martha Lou Lemmon Stohlmn, *The Story of Sweet Briar College* (Alumnae Association of Sweet Briar College, 1956), 171.
249. Stohlmn, *Story of Sweet Briar College*, 170.

Chapter 33

250. "Hollins Honors the University's Founder and Sustainers," Hollins University, February 28, 2017, https://www.hollins.edu/news/hollins-honors-universitys-founder-sustainers/.
251. Hollins College historical marker, Board of Supervisors of Roanoke County (marker no. A-79), 1978.
252. "Jamison, Susan Venable," obituaries, *The Roanoke* (VA) *Times*, September 22, 2020, 7.

Chapter 34

253. L.B. Taylor Jr., *Haunted Roanoke* (The History Press, 2013), 100.
254. Taylor Jr., *Haunted Roanoke*, 100.
255. "Patrick Henry's Family," Red Hill Patrick Henry National Memorial, https://www.redhill.org/patrick-henry/patrick-henrys-family/.
256. Isabella Ledonne, "Roanoke City Sees Increase in Homeless Population from Last Summer," WDBJ 7, July 31, 2023, https://www.wdbj7.com/2023/08/01/roanoke-city-sees-an-increase-homeless-last-summer/.
257. The Rescue Mission of Roanoke, https://rescuemission.net/.
258. Ralph Berrier Jr., "The Owners of Two Historic Roanoke Cemeteries Want to Give the Properties to the City—But the City Doesn't Want Them," *Cardinal News* (VA), February 21, 2023, https://cardinalnews.org/2023/02/21/the-owners-of-two-historic-roanoke-cemeteries-want-to-give-the-properties-to-the-city-but-the-city-doesnt-want-them/.
259. Alena R. Pirok, *The Common Uncanny: Ghostlore and the Creation of Virginia History* (University of South Florida, 2017), 7.
260. Pirok, *Common Uncanny*, 7.
261. The Rescue Mission of Roanoke.

Chapter 35

262. "Town of Christiansburg Sunset Cemetery Master Plan," New River Valley Regional Commission, 2014, https://www.christiansburg.org/166/Cemetery.
263. "Sunset Cemetery Master Plan," New River Valley Regional Commission.
264. "History of Sunset Cemetery," Christiansburg, Virginia, https://www.christiansburg.org/286/History-of-Sunset-Cemetery.
265. "Sisters in Black Disclose Weird Crime," *Knoxville* (TN) *Journal*, April 21, 1946.
266. Anna Strock, "These 5 Stories of Serial Killers in Virginia Will Leave You Terrified," Only in Your State, April 1, 2015, www.onlyinyourstate.com/virginia/5-serial-killers-in-virginia/.

267. Kevin Poff, cemeterian, personal correspondence, Town of Christiansburg, May 18, 2021.
268. Poff, personal correspondence.
269. "Exhibitions: Galleries at the Montgomery Museum," Montgomery Museum, www.montgomerymuseum.org.

Chapter 37

270. Carolyn Wilson, "A Town's 'Melting Pot' Cemetery Honored Miners from Many Cultures but Full into Disrepair. Supporters Want to Give It New Life," *Cardinal News* (VA), November 22, 2023, https://cardinalnews.org.
271. Wilson, "Town's 'Melting Pot.'"
272. "Bluefield 'Ghost' to Trouble No More," *The Roanoke Times*, September 19, 1930, 16.
273. "Bluefield 'Ghost,'" *The Roanoke Times*.

Chapter 38

274. Sherman Carmichael, *Mysterious Virginia* (The History Press, 2022), 55.

Chapter 39

275. Bud Phillips, "East Hill Cemetery Is the Most Haunted Place in the City of Bristol," *Bristol* (VA) *Herald Courier*, December 29, 2013, 22.
276. Phillips, "East Hill Cemetery Is the Most Haunted Place," 22.
277. Tom Netherland, "East Hill Cemetery Ghost Walk Highlight's Bristol's Former Residents," *Times News* (Kingsport, TN), October 18, 2022, https://www.timesnews.net/news/local-news/east-hill-cemetery-ghost-walk-highlights-bristols-former-residents/article_6c581e48-4e74-11ed-992b-d30e12d12aa3.html.
278. V.N. "Bud" Phillips, *Ghosts of Bristol* (The History Press, 2010), 19–20.
279. Phillips, *Ghosts of Bristol*, 30–31.

Chapter 40

280. Dock Boggs, "Oh, Death," *His Folkways Years, 1963-1968* (1998), https://folkways.si.edu/dock-boggs/oh-death-2/american-folk-old-time/music/track/smithsonian.
281. The song "Oh Death" is generally attributed to the musician and Baptist preacher Lloyd Chandler, but it was likely adapted from folk songs that already existed in the region.

Chapter 42

282. Cedar Hill Cemetery, https://covington.va.us/about-covington/facilities/cedar-hill-cemetery/.
283. "Claim Ghost Seen in Cedar Hill Cemetery," *The Covington Virginian*, July 2, 1930, 7.
284. "Ghost Seen in Cedar Hill," *The Covington Virginian.*
285. "Ghost Seen in Cedar Hill," *The Covington Virginian.*
286. "Ghost Seen in Cedar Hill," *The Covington Virginian.*
287. David Crosier, "The Ghost of Mrs. Jeter," *The Virginian Review*, August 27, 2021, https://virginianreview.com/24545/.
288. L.B. Taylor Jr., "Buried Alive—For Real!" in *The Ghosts of Virginia*, 4:215–17.
289. Troy Taylor, *Beyond the Grave* (Whitechapel Productions Press, 2001), 55.
290. Crosier, "Ghost of Mrs. Jeter."
291. Crosier, "Ghost of Mrs. Jeter."
292. "A Singular Invention," *The Abingdon Virginian*, September 11, 1868, 4.
293. Alexander Poots, "People Are Still Being Buried Alive," UnHerd, October 21, 2023, https://unherd.com/2023/10/people-are-still-being-buried-alive/.
294. Poots, "People Are Still Being Buried Alive."

Chapter 43

295. Thornrose Cemetery, https://thornrose.org/.
296. "Circus Folk Mark Grave of Eva Clark," *The (VA) News Leader*, September 14, 1923.
297. "Cemetery Ghost Turns Out to Be Just Monkey," *The Roanoke Times*, September 21, 1951, 2.
298. Aíne Murphy Norris, "Lore No More: Uncovering Eva Clark's Rightful Legacy," *Bandwagon: The Journal of the Circus Historical Society* 64, no 3 (2020): 32.
299. Norris, "Lore No More," 45.

Chapter 44

300. "Things That Go Bump in the Valley," *Living in Virginia*, season 3, episode 5, aired October 20, 2000, PBS, https://www.pbs.org/video/living-virginia-living-virginia-things-go-bump-valley/.
301. "Adam Wise Kersh to George P. Kersh, March 12, 1864," Valley Personal Papers, Library of Virginia, https://valley.lib.virginia.edu/papers/A0349.
302. Joshua Farnsworth, "1800's Archaeology Tour of Adam Kersh's Cabinet Shop," Wood and Shop, October 24, 2014, https://woodandshop.com/1800s-adam-kersh-workshop-archaeology-tour/.

Chapter 46

303. St. Paul Lutheran Church, https://stpaulstrasburgva.com/about/.
304. "Virginia Ghost Stories: The Balzer Huber House," *Southern Ghost Stories*, http://southernghoststories.com/virginia-ghost-stories-the-balzer-huber-house.
305. Tftaylo, "I Believe in Them Now (Ghosts in the Balzer Huber House), an Interview with Lavern F. Pitman, June 2005," published December 18, 2017, https://youtu.be/3ZFgP_NF5u8?si=fgvV-OW0kTQyE226.

Chapter 47

306. David Foley, personal correspondence, Prospect Hill Cemetery, July 17, 2024; "Prospect Hill Cemetery Association," *Richmond* (VA) *Dispatch*, July 15, 1872, 1.
307. "The Old Dominion," *The News and Advance* (Lynchburg VA), March 14, 1882, 3.
308. "Six Interesting Facts about Front Royal's Prospect Hill Cemetery," Discover Front Royal Virginia, October 30, 2022, https://www.discoverfrontroyal.com/blog/six-facts-about-front-royals-prospect-hill-cemetery.

Chapter 48

309. Mount Hebron Cemetery, https://mthebroncemetery.org/history/.
310. L.B. Taylor Jr., "The Phantom Mourner," in *The Big Book of Virginia Ghost Stories* (Globe Pequot, 2010), 147; Mac Rutherford, *Historic Haunts of Winchester* (The History Press, 2007), 18.
311. Taylor Jr., "Phantom Mourner," 147.
312. Rutherford, *Historic Haunts*, 91.

About the Author

Sharon Pajka, PhD, is a professor of English at Gallaudet University. She is the author of *Women Writers Buried in Virginia* (2021) and *The Souls Close to Edgar Allan Poe* (2023), a 2024 Saturday "Visiter" Award winner for "Adaptations of E.A. Poe's Life or Works." On the weekends, you can find her in the cemetery giving history tours or volunteering.

Visit us at
www.historypress.com

....